Cases for Intervention Planning

Cases for Intervention Planning

A *Source Book*

Molly R. Hancock, M.S.W., C.S.W.

Kenneth I. Millar, M.S.W., Ph.D.
*University of Arkansas
at Little Rock*

Nelson-Hall Publishers / Chicago

Project Editor: Rachel Schick
Cover Art: "Oak Leaves" by Sandra Principe

Library of Congress Cataloging-in-Publication Data

Hancock, Molly R.
    Cases for intervention planning : a source book / Molly R. Hancock
and Kenneth I. Millar.
        p. cm.
    Includes index.
    ISBN 0-8304-1301-4
    1. Social case work—Case studies.   2. Social case work—United
States—Case studies.   I. Millar, Kenneth I.   II. Title.
HV43.H313   1992
361.3′2—dc20   92-3758
                                                                              CIP

Manufactured in the United States of America

10 9 8 7 6 5 4 3 2 1

™ The paper used in this book meets the minimum requirements of American National Standard for Information Sciences—Permanence of Paper for Printed Library Materials, ANSI Z39.48-1984.

Contents

Contents

Preface

The cases in this book reflect the life situations of many clients with whom the authors and some of our colleagues have been privileged to work. All identifying information has been changed and each case has been significantly altered with respect to details and events. In many instances, the "real-life" cases served solely as rudimentary frames, around which we built fictional descriptions of situations and events.

In writing some of the cases, we consulted with colleagues in various fields of practice, and we wish to acknowledge the debt we owe to their insight, helpful interest, and ready cooperation in the project.

Bamber, Chris, B.S.W., Acting Income Maintenance Supervisor and formerly, Supervisor, Vocational Rehabilitation Services, Ministry of Community and Social Services, Province of Ontario, Sudbury, Ontario.

Bowes-Chezzi, Donna, B.S.W., Director, Genevra House for Battered Women, Y.W.C.A., Sudbury, Ontario.

Condratto, Brenda, General Counselor, Workers' Compensation Board, Province of Ontario, Sudbury, Ontario.

Damore-Petingola, Sheila, B.S.W., Social Worker, Psycho-Social Services, Northeastern Ontario Regional Cancer Centre. Formerly with the Intensive Rehabilitation Unit, Laurentian Hospital, Sudbury, Ontario.

DiNorcia, Linda, M.S.W., Director of Social Work, Laurentian Hospital, Sudbury, Ontario.

Holder, Lynne, B.S.W., Probation Officer, Juvenile Division, Probation and Parole, Province of Ontario, Sudbury, Ontario.

Klingen-Milligan, Amy, B.S.W., Probation Officer, Adult Division, Probation and Parole, Province of Ontario, Sudbury, Ontario.

Konarek, Barbara, M. Ed. At the time of our consultation and, until her untimely death from cancer in 1990, she was Special Education Consultant for the Sudbury Board of Education, Sudbury, Ontario. Ms. Konarek, adopted as a child, had independently undertaken a search for her birth mother and siblings. Subsequently, she helped many people, both adoptees and social workers, with the process and impact of searching and finding— or not finding—birth parents, both directly and through her sensitive and knowledgeable writings and public presentations.

Labelle, Michelle, B.S.W., Social Worker, Chronic Care Services and formerly, with Renal Dialysis Services, Laurentian Hospital, Sudbury, Ontario.

Millar, Patricia, L.C.S.W., Case Manager, Domiciliary Homeless Program, V.A. Medical Center, Department of Veteran's Affairs, Little Rock, AR.

Rasi, Geraldine, B.S.W., Coordinator, Crisis Program, Sudbury General Hospital of the Immaculate Heart of Mary, Sudbury, Ontario.

St. Onge, Joyce, B.A., Adoption Disclosure Services, Children's Aid Society of the Districts of Sudbury and Manitoulin, Sudbury, Ontario.

West, Lola, L.C.S.W., Coordinator, Adult Day Health Care Program, V.A. Medical Center, Department of Veteran's Affairs, Little Rock, AR.

Finally, the authors wish to acknowledge the contributions of the members of the Theory for Social Work Practice class, Fall/Spring 1988–89, School of Social Work, Laurentian University, Sudbury, Ontario; and the Foundations of Social Work Practice class, Fall, 1989, Department of Social Work, University of Arkansas at Little Rock. Many of the cases were used in these classes to teach assessment skills and intervention planning. The insightful comments and suggestions of these students helped the authors refine the cases and are greatly appreciated.

Molly Hancock
Sudbury, Ontario

Ken Millar
Little Rock, Arkansas

Introduction

This book contains thirty cases which describe various social problems that professional social workers encounter in their daily practice. They are drawn from the fields of child welfare, health, family services, vocational rehabilitation, mental health, and corrections. The cases are written from the perspective of an intake worker and are intended to challenge the student's ability to do an appropriate assessment of the problem and to propose an intervention plan.

The cases are drawn from the authors' practice experiences, and from numerous interviews conducted with professional social workers in a variety of practice settings. In some instances, direct requests were made to colleagues to develop cases from their practice in order to get as broad a range of cases as possible.

The book is aimed at undergraduate and graduate students taking courses in social work theory and practice. Since the cases deal with various aspects of the human condition and raise broader issues of social policy, the book could also be used in Human Behavior and the Social Environment and Social Policy courses. It is conceivable that an integrated approach could be developed where a case is approached from a policy, HBSE, and practice perspective simultaneously.

To the Student: On Learning by the Case Method

The cases found in this book are descriptions of situations which require the intervention of a professional social worker. They are written from the perspective of an intake worker who has seen the client(s), in most instances, only once. As such, they provide intake information and the worker's observations as a basis for bio-psycho-social case study and beginning assessment, leading to the development of an intervention plan.

The cases are designed so that you will need to determine what material is already present and what needs to be obtained in further contact. They will also provide you with the opportunity to examine and evaluate the worker's behavior, as well as his or her recording style and skill. Some of the cases offer an opportunity for evaluation of the worker's handling of various issues such as: use or misuse of authority, aggressiveness on the part of the client, whether the intervention was appropriate from an ethical and/or legal perspective, and so forth.

Case Analysis

These cases offer you a powerful learning vehicle. You must review the relevant facts, analyze and interpret them, reach some conclusion about the problem and its cause(s), and recommend some intervention. You will find that the cases will generate a variety of different positions even though everyone is looking at the same evidence. In addition, these different viewpoints will lead to different, but equally plausible, problem statements and proposed solutions.

As you study each of these cases, you will individually invest time making sense of the evidence, diagnosing the problem, and thinking of interventions. You will probably uncover some aspect of the case your classmates will overlook, and each of you will probably read identical pieces of information slightly differently. Based on your reading, thinking, and analysis, you will construct your own action plan, believe in its rightness, and, hopefully, come to class prepared to defend it.

However, the real learning in the case method comes not in isolation, but in group discussion and debate about the case in question. You should see yourself as an intimately invested participant who must rethink the validity of your individual analysis continually as the group discussion about the case unfolds. Thus, you will spend much time *thinking* during the case discussion because your point of view will be challenged by different views of identical facts. You may find that you must either defend your view publicly or abandon it, as the group moves in some direction not supported by your own analysis. You should strive not only toward understanding and assessment but also toward action and intervention. Keep in mind that analytic brilliance, even persuasively expressed, is totally useless unless somebody does something as a result.

You will find that more intense effort is required for case learning than from any other form of instruction. When you begin, you will attack problems by groping, and your undirected energy will sometimes lead you nowhere. However, in a short period of exposure to cases, a more focused and assured manner will set in that leads to firm and informed action regardless of the problem's fuzziness or the incompleteness of the facts. The reasons for these changes include the following:

1. From exposure to problems with no "right" answer, you are forced to formulate a personally workable approach to problem definition and formulation; and,

2. Repetitive exposure to these ambiguous problems has a remarkable confidence-building effect on those who eventually must deal with similar problems in professional practice. What psychologists call "a tolerance for ambiguity" is fostered directly by case learning. You will learn to drive toward specific actions in spite of incomplete information, uncertain circumstances, and unclear problems. Although this can sometimes provoke premature action, such a model is much more consistent with the way the "real world" works than is an insistence on complete information or unattainable certainty.

You will get the most out of these cases if you approach each one as if *you* were the intake worker. You will struggle to find a suitable analytical tool for the problem, and then invest effort in analyzing the data to reach a useful set of action recommendations. However in spite of this investment, you will be continually reminded that problems are ambiguous, and your classmates' ideas may be as worthy, or more so, than your own. In the best sense of the word, you should remain an "idea chef," constantly melding the best of your own with the best of your classmates' thoughts to reach a better understanding of the problem and its action requirements.

To the Instructor: On Teaching by the Case Method

There is no one "method" to teach with cases. You should use the cases according to your own style and preference. Some instructors may choose to provide a summary lecture to explain learnings; others may leave the students to ponder on their own. Some may structure their classes tightly; others may be rather free-flowing. The way the cases are used depends on your preference, the students' needs and expectations, and the context of the course.

Each case is a written description of a problem faced by a social worker. The description contains both opinions and facts and puts the student in the position of having to sort through the information, decide what the problems are, analyze and interpret them, and then decide what actions to take. In preparing for the case discussion, the student uses the concepts and theories that you have covered or are currently covering in your course and can be guided in preparing the case by assignment questions which you can give them in advance. We have deliberately not provided a set of discussion questions in order to give you maximum latitude in approaching the cases as you see fit. The study, assessment, and intervention planning of each of these cases can be undertaken using different tools and models of assessment and intervention, according to your preference and the orientation of your course.

In a case discussion, students struggle with the problems presented in the case, discuss and compare their analyses of the problems, and propose actions to resolve the problems. In this process, they have an opportunity to use course concepts, test their own assessment against those of other students, and learn from each other. In this respect, case discussions are similar to experiential exercises in that students become active participants in the learning process and responsible for the quality of their own learning.

We have found that the best way to structure the class is to divide it into work groups of five or six students. These groups each take responsibility for presenting the case during the class period. Part of your role, of course, is to weave individual contributions toward a group product that is somewhat different from and better than the sum of the individual analyses. The specifics of how you lead the discussion will depend on your own objectives for the class as well as your own personal teaching style.

We have found that students typically need some form of closure at the end of class. This may take the form of a brief summary or a more detailed presentation of your own analysis of the case. Some sort of wrap-up remarks at the end of class, however brief, are necessary, as is some "bridging" that relates the discussion to the next class.

PART ONE

SERVICES FOR CHILDREN

CHAPTER 1

Sexual Child Abuse: Jean Jarvis and Family

Agency:
Child Welfare Services in a medium-sized city (pop. 130,000).

Referral date:
January 20, 19xx.

Referral source:
Ms. Kay Partridge, School Nurse, Longwell Road Elementary School.

Family data:
Father: Kenneth Jarvis, age 35, born September 21, 19xx.
Mother: Jean Elmira Jarvis, age 31, born June 1, 19xx.
Children: Marie, age 8, born October 12, 19xx.
Joanne, age 7, born December 14, 19xx.

Note: Because of the sexual abuse aspect of this case, coupled with the gender and age of the children, it was decided that a female worker would be most appropriate.

Background

This case came to our agency from Longwell Road Elementary School. The school nurse was asked by the principal, Ms. Marcia Caprilano, to contact us. The teachers of both Marie and Joanne had consulted together and subsequently brought to Ms. Caprilano their concern about the pervasive "sadness and shrinking timidity" of these little girls. Marie is bright, and when her interest is caught does very good work. Joanne has been designated a "slow learner" and is in a special education class. Both teachers, who are experienced and are known

3

for their gentleness in their approach to their pupils, had tried to ask the children if something was bothering them. Although at first both girls said nothing was wrong, Joanne had later told her teacher that there were things "I mustn't talk about because I mustn't talk about dirty things."

The school nurse, Ms. Kay Partridge, contacted by the principal, had talked with both girls together, but both had again denied that anything was troubling them. However, she had visited the home by appointment, on January 19, 19xx, and talked with Mrs. Jarvis. Mrs. Jarvis had said that both girls had always been shy, and quieter than most children. She herself had always been very shy as a child. She attributed the girls' shyness to their living in an older neighborhood, where there were very few families with children the same ages as her girls. She had told Ms. Partridge that Mr. Jarvis' employment had been threatened recently by some changes at the mill where he worked as a shipping clerk, and she thought the girls might have become worried because they had heard her and their father talking about possible unemployment and money worries. Ms. Partridge stated that Mrs. Jarvis had said, "You know how kids pick up things, without understanding what's going on." Mrs. Jarvis had added, however, that she herself had not noticed anything unusual in her children's behavior. She did tell the nurse that the girls' trouble might be that their father is "rather strict" with them. Before Ms. Partridge could ask her to elaborate, Mrs. Jarvis said that she would talk this over with him, and if they thought they needed any further help they would call the nurse.

Ms. Partridge had told her that in view of the school's expressed concern, she would call our agency and have us contact the family. She stressed that our role was to help families with different kinds of difficulties and since it seemed that the girls were not doing very well, some help now with whatever was troubling them might prevent worse problems later on. She noted that one of our workers would likely call to make an appointment to come and see her and her husband. Ms. Partridge noticed that Mrs. Jarvis said in a strangely quiet, almost resigned way, "Perhaps that would be for the best."

The home was visited on January 30, 19xx, and the parents signed a consent form for a psychological assessment by the agency psychologist. The children were brought to the agency on the following day, January 31st. During the latter session, both children told of frequent sexual abuse by their father, while their mother was out shopping or at her bingo night. He had fondled their genitals, forced them to perform oral sex on him, and made them bring him to orgasm with his penis between their legs. Marie said this had started when she was about three years old and had continued up to the present.

Marie said her father had told her that this was what loving fathers did, but it was always "their secret" and that no one must ever know, especially their mother, because she might be "jealous," and then he would have to punish her for not understanding how much he loved his girls.

The agency immediately informed the police, who also interviewed the children in the presence of our sexual abuse team worker. Mr. Jarvis was arrested immediately and was arraigned on February 3rd, remanded without bail, and formally charged in court on February 24th.

In the course of the investigation and in giving evidence in court, Mrs. Jarvis admitted that she had known that her husband was "playing with" the girls; that she had thought it was "nothing really bad" and that they were "making something out of nothing." She had pretended not to believe them when they tried to tell her about it, thinking that this was the best way to deal with it. Mr. Jarvis had been physically abusive to her frequently since their first year of marriage, and she was terrified of his violence. She had told the children more than once that they must never talk about "such dirty things," and felt she could not tell anyone else because perhaps they were just "making it all up."

On March 19th, Mr. Jarvis was sentenced to two years in jail. In light of the evidence Mrs. Jarvis gave, indicating her difficulty in protecting the girls from their father's sexual abuse or herself from his violence, it was agreed in a conference between the child abuse team and family services that both she and the girls needed help with the damaging effects of these experiences as well as the aftermath of their father's committal. Accordingly, I arranged to interview Mrs. Jarvis to discuss this, hoping to obtain her voluntary cooperation in a service plan.[1]

Interview in Office with Mrs. Jarvis, April 2, 19xx

Mrs. Jarvis' appearance had changed noticeably since I had last seen her two weeks ago. She had always looked neat and well-groomed, dressed in rather conservative style and had, I thought, looked somewhat older than her age. There had been a dramatic change in her

---

1. In some jurisdictions, an option may be available to obtain a court order of supervision for a specified period of time.

appearance. She had had her mid-brown hair dyed bright blonde and quite elaborately styled. She was wearing bright red lipstick and nail polish and wore large brilliant drop earrings with a matching necklace. She carried a bright red shoulder bag, which looked new. I said the blonde hair color suited her very well, and she smiled and said it made a "nice change."

I explained to her that I had wanted to see her because we have found that children who have been sexually abused usually need some special help with getting over the experience, and that we believed that we could help her help the children over this. I said I also recognized that she had had a very difficult life with Mr. Jarvis and that this had undoubtedly affected her in many ways, and I would like to help her rebuild her life and plan for the future for herself and the girls.

Mrs. Jarvis replied that while she had appreciated the agency's help over the past two months, she and the girls were "just fine" now that it was all over. She had moved into an apartment her sister had located for her. Her application for social assistance had been approved and she feels she will be able to manage although it will be tight. The girls felt good about going to a new school where she hoped no one knew anything about their father. Joanne seemed to miss her teacher at Longwell Road but Mrs. Jarvis feels that she'll "get over that in no time."

Marie misses her special school friend, Heather, but Mrs. Jarvis has told her it was best if she didn't see Heather anymore, although the girl's mother had called to invite Marie to visit. Mrs. Jarvis has told Marie that those people (i.e., Heather's parents) might "get funny ideas" about her dad being in jail. She has told Marie that she will soon make new friends at the new school as long as she didn't "mope around" about Heather.

I asked her if the girls had talked to her about how they felt about their dad going to jail, or about the experience of going to court. Mrs. Jarvis said they hadn't, at least, "not really." I asked how she meant "not really" and she went on to say she believes it is best for them "not to dwell on those things." She feels that such young children soon forget unpleasant experiences and feels sure they will soon "cheer up" if she tells them just to forget all about it, now that it's over. She feels that our continuing to "oversee" (her word) them, will only make it harder for her to help them forget it all and to "put it all right out of their minds." My visits would be a constant reminder of "things best forgotten."

I told Mrs. Jarvis that I could not completely agree with her certainty that the girls would forget all about their experiences so easily. It had been my experience, and that of others working with sexually abused children, that it was healthier in the long run if children were allowed, even encouraged, to talk about their feelings, and to express what had troubled, and continued to trouble them. In this way they got over it, whereas trying to push it out of their minds didn't work. The feelings would "fester underground," so to speak, and create difficulties for them later on, when it would be more difficult to help them deal with it. I said I knew she believed she was doing the best for her children, but that I had a responsibility to tell her that our experience has shown that this is not the best way to go about it.

Mrs. Jarvis asked me if I had any children of my own. I said I didn't and I wondered aloud if she felt that meant I didn't know very much about kids. She didn't mean to be rude, she said, but after all, "You can't beat experience, can you?" I said no, indeed, but that I had had ten years of experience working with abused children and their parents, and backed by my professional studies, this had taught me quite a lot about these particular children. Mrs. Jarvis smiled in a rather patronizing way and said she supposed she couldn't argue with that, and that, in fact, she had been thinking of going back to school herself in order to train for a decent job. She is worried about how to manage without Mr. Jarvis' paycheck. She had worked as a waitress before marriage, and for a couple of years afterwards, but she couldn't go back to evening work like that while the girls were still so young. She hadn't liked the work, anyway, because so many of the men customers were "coarse and objectionable."

I said that I would be very glad to help her look at various choices about available courses leading to more rewarding employment, and that I felt she was wise to look ahead for herself and the girls in terms of planning for their lives after Mr. Jarvis' release from jail. Mrs. Jarvis said angrily that just when she had got away from all that misery and was trying to put it all out of her mind, I started talking about when he gets out. She asked if I called that "helpful" and she started to cry. I said I hadn't meant to push her, only to commend her for looking now at her own career plans, and to support her in such planning.

Mrs. Jarvis began to cry bitterly, saying I could have no idea what she had been through and how hard all this with the girls had been for her. It had stirred up "terrible things" that "didn't bear thinking about." No one knew how hard it had been for her to live with Mr. Jarvis' beatings. She said I was smart not to get married, that men treat women like "shit," even "tiny little girls." How could I say that talking about such terrible things was good for a person? I said I knew that it could be scary at first, but talking about the things that terrify us did, in my experience, begin to take away the power they have to frighten us. It gave us the power to face up to what was real and to put the past in the past where it belongs, instead of dragging it around with us in fear and dread of it "getting out of the bag."

Mrs. Jarvis looked up at me sharply when I said that and I felt my phrase had touched a nerve. She dried her eyes and said she hadn't meant to be "rude"—only that no one knew what she had been through. I agreed that only she knew what it had been like for her. She quickly closed her purse, and got up. She picked up her jacket and said, almost sharply, "Well, when shall I bring the girls in?" We made an appointment for three days hence and I said we would talk then about a contract for service[2] and she agreed.

2. As previously noted, supervision may be mandated by the court in some jurisdictions.

CHAPTER 2

Child Abuse—Emotional Neglect: Eva Jones and Family

Agency:
Family and Children's Services of Lakesford, a medium-sized industrial city (pop. 150,000).

Referral date:
October 19, 19xx.

Referral source:
Mrs. Kusniak, guidance teacher, Cameronsville High School.

Home location:
Rural village of Belisle, 10 miles from Cameronsville, which is 40 miles from Lakesford.

Family data:

Father:	George, aged 35, left the family when Mrs. Jones was four months pregnant with Gary. Present whereabouts unknown.
Mother:	Eva, age 34, born May 8, 19xx.
Children:	Jeannette, age 16, born January 20, 19xx.
	Anne, age 14, born April 23, 19xx.
	Stella, age 13, born February 19, 19xx.
	Gary, age 10, born June 7, 19xx.

Presenting Problem

The referral concerns fourteen year old Anne Jones, a grade 9 student who school officials believe is abnormally quiet and withdrawn. Mrs. Kusniak, who made the referral, described her as a "sad child." While there are no discipline problems of a disruptive nature, Anne has periods of staring out of the classroom window, "almost as if she didn't know where she was." Assigned classroom work is rarely completed. Mrs. Kusniak reports that Anne tests at slightly above average ability with good potential for mathematics and science.

The following additional information was also received from the referral source. The girl's mother is Mrs. Eva Jones, a single parent, who works at the Valleyview Golf and Country Club in Belisle. Mrs. Kusniak believes that the mother has a boyfriend and has heard from friends in Belisle that "she has no time for the children." There are three other children in the family: Jeannette, age sixteen, a bright student who was doing well in school but quit on her sixteenth birthday; Stella, a seriously retarded girl, age thirteen, who cannot speak or walk and is not toilet trained; and Gary, age ten, whom Mrs. Kusniak knew little about.

First Contact

I happened to be in Belisle the day after we received the referral and went to the Jones' home without a prior appointment. Jeannette was at home with Stella but I was not invited in. I identified myself and left my card. I telephoned at the first opportunity the next morning, spoke to Mrs. Jones, and explained the reason for the contact. An appointment was set for the following afternoon at the Jones' home.

First Interview

Mrs. Jones has no idea where Mr. Jones is, and has no wish to find out. She was frank about her background. She was married at age seventeen because she was pregnant and her parents and George's "gave us no choice." She was barely four months pregnant with Gary when he left. The marriage had been stormy throughout and Mrs. Jones "always felt George resented having to get married and blamed me and the kids for stopping him from getting ahead."

She works as a waitress in the dining room at the Golf and Country Club and makes enough "to keep things going." In answer to my question as to whether she has ever considered social assistance, she replied that she could never accept "charity" again. She had been on welfare when her husband first left and spoke bitterly of the humiliation and the inadequacy of the allowance. She would tell me nothing about her financial position, stating, "I'm not asking for anything and it's none of your business."

She has a boyfriend who is chief bartender at the golf club and who drives her to and from work each day. He is separated from his wife and neither Mrs. Jones nor he have any thoughts about marriage.

Her attitude towards the community of Belisle and to people in general is that they are, without exception, untrustworthy, two-faced, out to put you down, etc. For these reasons, she discourages the children from mixing with, or getting friendly with, the neighborhood children.

Response to Contact

At this first interview, Mrs. Jones was very cold and guarded and, at times, quite aggressive and hostile. Although she invited me to sit down, she remained standing and moving around the room for the first several minutes. She did not sit down until she started talking about the people of Belisle. At the time of the interview, Stella was sitting in a playpen, playing with some sort of ring-toy. Jeannette sat on a low stool near the playpen. During the interview, Anne and Gary came home from school. Anne stood near the stairs to the second floor and Gary sat on the sofa beside his mother.

Mrs. Jones was very angry about being "reported" to the agency. School teachers, public health nurses, and social workers, all have, in ascending order, the very worst characteristics of "people" as described above. I said that she "must have had some lousy experiences with social workers to feel that way," and she said, "You better believe it." She added that she was aware that this was my way of "tricking" her into saying things about her life that were "nobody's business."

In connection with the boyfriend, Mrs. Jones said she knew I had talked to the neighbors so there was no point in trying to lie about him. I stated that I had not done so and added that I didn't feel it was right to go behind someone's back. Mrs. Jones asked sarcastically if I really expected her to believe that, to which I responded that I hoped she would believe I was telling her the truth. After the children came home from school, Mrs. Jones attacked me less, but in general, her anger and bitterness persisted.

Mrs. Jones appears to be conscientious about the physical care of the children, but I wondered how much affection she was capable of giving them. She seemed at times insensitive or indifferent to their feelings. At one point, I tried to involve Anne in conversation, but she did not answer. Her mother said shrilly, "Can't you answer, you dummy?" At this point, Anne's eyes filled with tears and she went slowly up the stairs. I felt that Mrs. Jones was very threatened by this incident. Her voice was shrill and shaky as she told me that Anne was like that "sometimes" with strangers. However, she didn't know why the school was so concerned, since "some kids are just quiet by nature."

There was a gleam of tenderness in Mrs. Jones' attitude towards Stella which, on the occasion of this visit at least, was missing from any exchanges with her other children. She called Stella "baby" and patted her on the shoulder a number of times. She left me in no doubt that she would never "put Stella away," and it was her job to "look after the poor little thing." She repeated several times that Stella had not asked to be born "that way." My attempts to recognize that Stella's care must nevertheless be quite a burden on her were sharply and angrily dismissed. "It might be to some people who only want their own selfish way, but Stella is my child as much as the others." When I attempted to ask about Stella's early development, Mrs. Jones changed the subject, and I did not see any purpose in pursuing this subject at the time.

Mrs. Jones "supposes" she must have more visits from a social worker as it "will only be held against me if I refuse." As far as she was concerned, she was doing her best, her kids were well cared for, and were better than most of the other kids in the community.

I explained the role and responsibility of the agency in such a case and emphasized the school's genuine concern about Anne. I also explained to Mrs. Jones that a worker would be out to see her in the next week or so and would telephone beforehand to find a convenient time.

Observations

The children all appear neatly dressed and well-groomed. Mrs. Jones herself is well-groomed, with fine features, medium height, and a slim build. Housekeeping standards appear excellent, although structurally and in furnishings, the home is rather shabby and run-down looking.

School attendance is regular and there are no behavior problems. When Jeannette quit school at sixteen, this was fully supported by the mother, who stated that she (Jeannette) was "getting a lot of big ideas about college and taking up a profession," and that it was "high time she came down to earth and started making herself useful." Mrs. Jones feels that Anne may as well quit at sixteen as well, since "she hasn't the brains to go on," and, in any case, "too much education only spoils kids for earning a living later."

The children are very well-mannered but seemed subdued and

12

lacking in spontaneity of any kind on the occasion of the one visit. The children, according to the mother, are never unruly, who added fiercely, "No one can say my kids aren't good." All the children share in home responsibilities but only Jeannette and the mother care for Stella.

CHAPTER 3

Emotional Child Abuse: James McLeod

Agency:
Child Welfare Authority in a medium-sized industrial city (pop. 125,000).

Referral date:
November 15, 19xx.

Referral source:
Mrs. Joanne Moffatt, next-door neighbor of the McLeod family.

Family data:
Father: Malcolm McLeod, age 44, born July 1, 19xx.
Mother: Patricia McLeod, age 43, born February 19, 19xx.
Children: Roderick, age 16, born January 25, 19xx.
Douglas, age 14, born March 8, 19xx.
James, age 7, born September 24, 19xx.

Presenting Problem

Mrs. Moffatt is very concerned about the behavior of Jimmy McLeod. She said it has been very difficult for her to get to the point of coming to us, because her husband says she shouldn't interfere in the lives of their neighbors, but finally she simply had to—she couldn't stand to see what was happening anymore.

Jimmy actually terrorizes the other children in the townhouse complex where they live. He "comes out fighting" in the morning, and it is just the same after school. She feels he could really be a danger to the other children as he "just picks up anything," rocks, a baseball bat, once a sharp stake, and hits or throws it at anyone who gets in his way.

Mrs. Moffatt says it has deeply distressed her and her husband how Mr. McLeod treats Jimmy. He "seems to have no time for the little fellow" and will never take him on outings with the older boys. She even heard one of the older boys ask his father if Jimmy could go fishing with them, but the father refused, saying in front of Jimmy, "He hasn't got the brains to fish." Another time she heard this man ask Jimmy, "How did we get a dumb kid like you?"

Mr. McLeod once told Mrs. Moffatt's husband, "His mother would make a namby-pamby out of that kid, if I didn't take a firm hand."

Mrs. Moffatt gave her name and address, and although she hopes it will not "come out" that she has called us, she is concerned enough that she feels she must take that risk. She has talked to the parents of some of the other children in the complex, but they "don't want any trouble" and prefer to tell their children not to play with Jimmy.

Intake Interview

Mr. and Mrs. McLeod came to the office for an appointment and said they welcomed our concern. In the previous week, Jimmy had beaten up a child on the school playground, and the teacher had suggested to them that Jimmy needed help. They did not ask who had called us.

Mr. McLeod is in a middle-management position in an insurance firm. Mrs. McLeod is a registered nurse, but has not worked outside the home since Jimmy was born. They had not planned to have any more children after Douglas, but Jimmy was "an accident."

Mr. McLeod took the lead in the interview, and often replied to my questions even though I had directed them to his wife. He said that Jimmy was "different" from the other boys even when he was little. Mrs. McLeod said that even as a baby he was "cranky and demanding," whereas the others had been "such good babies."

Mr. McLeod said he and his wife had separated for about six months three years ago, but that it was "all over nothing, really," and they had put that behind them when they reconciled. Mrs. McLeod said nothing at this point, and I noticed that she looked out of the window while her husband made this statement.

Mr. McLeod says he really would be glad of our help. He has felt all along that there was something mentally wrong with Jimmy and that he hopes now we can find a psychiatrist who understands "mental deficiency" and can help them get the kind of treatment Jimmy needs. Perhaps he should be in a "special home for kids like that."

I explained that our service plan would be to include the whole family, as Jimmy's difficulties were clearly affecting everyone. This has been found to be the most effective way to help families. With family interviews, all the members of the family can be enlisted to cooperate in working to change things, and the burden does not just fall on the parents. Moreover, if everyone hears what is said, and everyone has a chance to be heard, all family members feel more secure and more involved in working to make things better.

Mr. McLeod wondered if this was just my "bright idea" or if it had been tried anywhere else. I explained that the principle of whole family involvement has been developing gradually since the sixties and that it has been conclusively found to be more helpful than just seeing one or two family members separately. Mrs. McLeod said she had seen something about it on TV.

Mr. McLeod was clearly still doubtful and suggested that I was not focusing sufficiently on Jimmy's "mental problem." He asked "with respect" what were my professional qualifications? I indicated my B.A. and M.S.W. degrees on the wall near him and my certificate of professional registration.[1]

I also told him that I had had seven years' experience with this agency, and that consultation with senior staff was always available to me.

Mr McLeod said he guessed he couldn't argue with all that. I said that as we worked together, I would rely on him and all the family members to speak up about what they didn't understand or found unhelpful. It was important that we worked together honestly and openly to find a way to resolve their difficulties.

They agreed to a family appointment two weeks from today.

---

1. This may vary in different jurisdictions, i.e., certification or licentiate in a professional state, provincial or national association or college.

CHAPTER 4

Physical Child Abuse: Hank Peters and Family

Agency:
Child Welfare Services in a medium-sized industrial city (pop. 100,000).

Referral date:
October 16, 19xx.

Referral source:
Mrs. Carla Tomassi, by phone to emergency service, approximately 8:20 p.m.

Family data:
Father: "Hank" (Hans) Peters, age 23, born August 6, 19xx.
Mother: Jeannette Monroe, age 22, born November 30, 19xx.
Children: Tammy Lynne Monroe, age 4, born September 15, 19xx.
Bruce Peters, age 3, born January 17, 19xx.

Intake interviews:
1. With Mr. and Mrs. Tomassi at their home, Oct. 16, 19xx.
2. With father, Hank Peters, Oct. 17, 19xx.
3. With father, Hank Peters, and mother, Jeannette Monroe, October 22nd, 19xx.

Presenting Problem

Mrs. Carla Tomassi had agreed to care for these two children, aged four and three years respectively, for three or four days while their mother was in hospital for an exploratory D & C and tests. She has known the family as neighbors for about six months. Hank and Jean-

17

nette had brought the children to her home at about 1:30 p.m. en route to the hospital. Jeannette had told her both children had fallen down the basement stairs earlier that day, but apart from being bruised they were not badly hurt.

Upon undressing the children, at bedtime, Mrs. Tomassi had found welts and bruises on both children, and had called the agency, as she was suspicious whether such injuries could have been caused by a fall. Mr. and Mrs. Tomassi are valued former foster parents of this agency. Mrs. Tomassi took what she called a "leave of absence" from fostering when she became pregnant with her youngest child, now eight months old.

On my arrival, she gently took off the children's pajamas and showed me that both had livid bruises and welts across their backs, from the shoulders almost to their knees. Tammy's appeared to be more livid, and she, unlike Bruce, had old, yellowing bruises on her upper arms and one cheek.

Although I was reluctant to put more stress on the children, the on-call supervisor agreed with me that for the protection of all concerned, I should take them to the emergency room at the hospital. Furthermore, I should formally take the children into our care, but could leave them with the Tomassi family overnight (they being known to us as reliable caregivers). I was, of course, obligated to let the parents know of this action.

At the emergency room I was fortunate to find not only the on-call physician, but a pediatrician as well. Both doctors were quite definite that the welts could not have been caused by a fall, although some of the bruises possibly could have been. The bruises on Tammy's upper arms were clearly in the pattern of an adult hand-grip. Dr. V. (the pediatrician) further pointed out a couple of places, on both children, where the skin was almost broken at the edge of the welts. This indicated, in his view, the use of some "edged" instrument. It was his opinion that this was likely a belt. When he asked the children what had happened, they both whispered, "We were real bad."

It was by then too late to talk to Jeannette, so I wrote her a note, which I gave to the nurse on duty, expressing our great concern over the children's injuries. (The hospital where I had taken the children was the same one where she was hospitalized for her tests.) I also assured her that no legal action would be taken without her and Hank's full knowledge, but that the children would remain in our care for the time being.

After returning the children to the Tomassis, I tried to locate Hank Peters at his home, but there was no one there. I wrote him a similar note, making an appointment for him to come to the office next morning, and left it at the home.

Mr. and Mrs. Tomassi were instructed to call the agency immediately if anyone should arrive at their home, or attempt to remove the children from their care.

Further Information from this Contact

I learned that Mrs. Tomassi had met Jeannette at a neighborhood Avon demonstration. At that time, Mrs. Tomassi was still fostering for the agency, and she and Jeannette had talked about fostering. Later, as the weather got warmer, they used to meet in the park with their children, and they had visited in each other's houses for coffee a few times. Mrs. Tomassi told me that she had often observed how very well-behaved the Peters' children were, considering their age. They never forgot to say "please" and "thank you," and always said "excuse me"—even Bruce—when they passed between two adults talking. The Tomassis had never met Hank.

Interview with Hank Peters

Mr. Peters, a fair-haired young man of medium height and slight build, came promptly for his appointment.

He tried at first to laugh off our concern and the "busy-body interference" of Mrs. Tomassi and myself. He remarked to me that it was too bad I didn't have anything better to do on weekends than poke my nose in where I had no business. He referred to a "couple of spankings" he had given the children on "Thursday, or maybe Friday," before Jeannette went into the hospital, but he made no mention of any fall downstairs, and neither did I.

He made it clear that in his view children of that age must be "spanked" for misbehavior, and they must "learn who's the boss." In reply to my question, he said the worst of their misbehavior was bed-wetting and soiling their pants, even in the daytime. They had both been "hard to train" and were exceptionally "stubborn and strong-willed." He feels that he and Jeannette have got to "win the battle." You couldn't let kids get away with such "defiance" or they would walk all over you. Several times he referred to the importance of "who's the boss."

I told him that on the basis of my observations and Dr. V.'s report we would be taking the matter to court, and that he should make arrangements, either through his own resources or through

Legal Aid, for a lawyer to represent them. At this he became very angry. He stood up and shouted threats at the agency, at me, and at the Tomassis. He threatened to bring a lawsuit that would "put the agency out of business for good," that would discredit me and force the Tomassis to "pay up" or he would take everything they ever owned. He yelled that it was pretty low down of me to make a "big case" so I would look good, taking children away from a devoted mother who was "fighting for her life in the hospital."

I said I wanted to see him and Jeannette together before the first court hearing, which would be on October 21st, and he said I could certainly count on that, provided "the poor girl isn't back in the hospital with a breakdown because of you!"

Further Developments

Following this interview, the court conference committee on child abuse cases met and determined that while it appeared that the children had certainly been inappropriately disciplined, bringing charges against the couple was not appropriate. Rather, it was determined to request the court for a relatively brief period of temporary wardship. During this period the children would remain in foster care and the parents would attend a parents' group, as well as work personally with a Family Service Worker on the child abuse team to help them develop more normal expectations of the children, and to learn new and appropriate methods of discipline. Three months was the suggested time period.

October 19, 19xx

Mr. Paul Lockridge, lawyer for the Peters, called. I explained to him the evidence on which we were going to court, and the recommendations we would bring as described in the notes above. At first he lectured me on the agency's "inflexibility" in not allowing for cultural differences in childrearing. He stated that Mr. Peters was brought up in Germany, and in our kind of community there was surely room for variations in discipline. I described the condition of the children, reminded him of their young age, and the "misbehavior" that Mr. Peters had told me was the cause of this "discipline." Mr. Lockridge became less aggressive at this point, and grudgingly conceded that some re-education of these parents "might" be appropriate and necessary. However, he believed that three months was far too long, and he said he would oppose this. He also stated that he would insist on regular and frequent visitation by the parents. I agreed that in this case we would also be recommending such visitation, but that we would hold to recommending three months of care. I invited him to be present at my scheduled interview with Mr. Peters and Ms. Monroe, and he said he would talk to them about this, as he didn't know if they should see me again before the court hearing.

Hank and Jeannette cancelled their appointment, on the advice of Mr. Lockridge. It was arranged that I would serve them with the notice of hearing at his office, and in his presence. At this meeting, I explained the precise purpose of the hearing, our proposed recommendations, and the reasons why we felt these would be beneficial for their family as a whole. Both parents were very quiet, and Mr. Lockridge was very understanding and helpful to them throughout this process. They agreed with his contention that three months was far too long for the children to be away from them, and were reassured that he was going to fight this for them. I told them that regular and frequent visits were to be part of our recommendations.

Court Decision

The children were committed to agency care for three months. They could be returned to their parents before the expiration of this order, at the discretion of the agency, depending upon the parents' cooperation with the parenting program and regular contact with the family worker of the child abuse team.

Background Information

Jeannette

Jeannette was adopted in infancy by Harvey and Leonora Monroe, who had one child of their marriage, Jason, now age twenty-eight. He was born June 16, 19xx.

Jeannette says she never felt she really belonged in her adoptive family. She could never measure up to their high standards of behavior, social graces, and so forth. She suffered unfavorable comparison with Jason continually, his good looks (he strongly resembled his mother), school grades, singing voice, etc. Although she felt her father was a little kinder than her mother, whom she experienced as cold, strict and unbending, his kindness only showed when mother was not at home. For example, his giving her a little extra spending money for herself was "our little secret, OK?" However in terms of good behavior, manners, tidiness, etc., he was just as strict as her mother.

Jeannette once asked her mother, "Why did you adopt me?" The mother replied, "Dad so much wanted a little girl."

After a stormy adolescence, Jeannette ran away from home at age seventeen and started living with a man, age thirty-five, separated from his wife. He promised to marry her when he could afford to get a divorce. After six months, when she told him she was pregnant, he "slapped her around" and told her she was a lousy little whore trying to trap him into marriage for her own benefit. He threw some of her things into a suitcase and drove her to her girlfriend's, telling her to stay out of his life forever if she knew what was good for her. Jeannette was determined to keep her baby and did so. After her daughter was born she was able to obtain subsidized housing and went on social assistance. Tammy, her daughter, was almost two years old when Jeannette met Hank.

Hank

Hank's parents emigrated from Germany 28 years ago.

Family data:

Father:	Guenther, born 19xx.
Mother:	Hulda, born 19xx.
Children:	Fred, age 41, born 19xx.
	Hulda, age 39, born 19xx.
	Tom, age 36, born 19xx.
	Hanne (Honey), age 34, born 19xx.
	Hans (Hank), age 23, born 19xx.

All the children were born in Germany except Hank. Both parents were killed in a car crash in 19xx. Hank, at the time, was eight years old. He remained in the family home, which was maintained by Hulda, Tom, and Honey, until Hulda married and took him to live with her and her husband a year after his parents' death. When Hulda's first child was born, Hank went to live with Fred and his wife, but this did not work out happily and after one year he went to live with Tom, who was newly married.

In all Hank lived with one or other of his siblings until he was eighteen, the details being as follows: age eight to nine at family home; age nine to eleven with Hulda and husband; age eleven to twelve with Fred and wife; age twelve to fourteen with Tom and wife; age fourteen to fifteen with Fred and wife; age fifteen to eighteen with Hulda and husband.

At age eighteen he went out to board on his own. He married at age twenty. His wife was twenty-five, a cook in a hospital, and pregnant at the time of marriage. Six months after the marriage, a boy, Bruce, was born. Hank said his wife treated Bruce as if "he was a real nuisance," and she "couldn't wait to get him with a girlfriend to babysit so's she could go back to work." At this time Hank was working at Jaynes' Steel, and making, in his words, "enough to get by." About twelve months later he learned that his wife had had an abortion, or an "induced miscarriage," with a girlfriend's help, and without his knowledge. He had beaten her up. Asked to explain, his words were, "I slapped her around real good so she'd know I was the boss." She left him and Bruce, who was then eleven months old.

He then took Bruce to board with Honey and her husband, and was living with them when he met Jeannette on New Year's two years ago. Bruce was not quite a year old when they met. They started living together shortly thereafter.

Hank described his many moves by saying, "I lived with whichever of the family would put up with me." He said he had plenty of "good lickings" and felt they hadn't done him any harm. At the first interview after the court hearing, he continued, though in a somewhat less blustering way, to argue that we were making "a big thing out of a little spanking," and quoted his lawyer as saying that the agency "had to take on a bleeding heart attitude toward kids because they get their money by having kids in foster homes." In this interview, Jeannette said she believed the children soiled and wet themselves "to be mean" and "to get back at her and Hank."

CHAPTER 5

Child Mental Health: Robert (Bobby) Boulton

Agency:
Children's Mental Health Services, in Cameronsville, a medium-sized industrial city (pop. 120,000).

Referral date:
November 15, 19xx.

Referral source:
Ms. Marg Zavitz, School Nurse at Maplewood School (by phone).

Family data:
   Father: Robert Boulton, age 33, born July 1, 19xx.
  Mother: Jennifer Boulton, age 32, born July 14, 19xx.
Children: Robert (Bobby), age 8, born August 20, 19xx.
               Mary Ann, age 6, born November 5, 19xx.
               Patricia, age 3, born June 16, 19xx.

Presenting Problem

Bobby Boulton is a student in third grade at Maplewood School. Since the beginning of the school year, he has been increasingly involved in fights with other children, both in the school playground and, according to his parents, on the street at home. Ms. Zavitz quoted Bobby's homeroom teacher as saying that he seemed to come to school "with a chip on his shoulder," just spoiling for a fight with anyone. His teacher from the previous year states that he was not an aggressive child in second grade.

Ms. Zavitz had visited the parents at the school's request and had talked with Mrs. Boulton. She found that the parents were very concerned, and noted that the school has had a good impression of them as conscientious and cooperative. Bobby had done well academically in second grade, but is not doing as well as expected in third grade. His teacher has told the parents that Bobby often tries to find a way to put off going out at recess. His mother says he doesn't want to go outside to play after school or on weekends and she has to "drive" him outdoors.

Intake Interview

The first interview took place in the family home. On the day before our scheduled appointment, Mr. Boulton sprained his knee and could not drive. I felt this gave me the opportunity to see the whole family in their home (perhaps also less threatening to Bobby) and asked if I might visit them there. They readily agreed.

Although they seemed to have done their best to reassure Bobby that they had not sought our help because he was "bad," he hung his head during most of the interview and did not respond to my attempts to involve him with anything more than shrugs and monosyllables.

I learned that after approximately seven months of unemployment (unemployment is 9 percent in Cameronsville at present), Mr. Boulton had obtained a job at a service station on the Lakesford Highway. The proprietor is a brother of Mr. Boulton's former supervisor at Carlton Steel. He started working at the service station in mid-August.

"I'm one of the lucky ones," he said, "No one else on our street is working." He continued (rather loudly), "Others could be working, but they're not hustling." He, on the other hand, is a "hustler," and "if the neighbors are jealous, that's their problem." To this last comment, he added quickly that he didn't really think his neighbors were envious. "They know the job just happened along for me," and "It hasn't made any difference to most of our friends and neighbors." At this he looked to Mrs. Boulton for confirmation. Her eyes filled with tears and she grabbed Patricia, who was then passing between her mother and me, and started to straighten the youngster's T-shirt and jeans.

In reply to my question about playmates, Mary Ann said that Bobby had told her not to play with her friend Cheryl anymore. "I'm not supposed to say why," she stated. I wondered aloud if it was because Cheryl's brother and Bobby had had a fight but Bobby shook his head defiantly and he said, "No, it's something else." He then glared disgustedly at Mary Ann, who hung her head.

I explained to the family that our agency does help with difficulties such as they were having, and that I was very glad they were so ready and willing to work on this, since their cooperation and understanding meant we were more than halfway there. Our job, I explained, was to help a family look at and talk over what was troubling and hurting them, and to figure out together what could be done about it; that our experience and a lot of research in children's mental health has clearly shown that when the whole family works together, good results are obtained in resolving such difficulties. Mr. Boulton said, smiling uncertainly, that he guessed there were other people that had problems besides them. I said, yes indeed, and commented that if they were the only family to have difficulty like this there wouldn't be a need for a children's mental health service in this area.

I explained that I would not be their therapist, and that because we had a staff member off sick and were having to rearrange work schedules, I couldn't give them a name today. However, I assured them that I would phone them as soon as I knew who it would be, and hoped this could be within two weeks. Recognizing that this was difficult for them, and that starting over with someone new might not be easy, I told them I would be talking with whomever it would be, and that he or she would have all the information they had given me.

Mr. Boulton expressed surprise that it might be a man. He thought "only women did this kind of work." I explained that we had both men and women on staff as therapists and that we all had the same kind of professional education and training. I said I believed that once they got to know the new worker, they would find they could talk with him or her openly and comfortably about the difficulty.

They agreed that they would wait for my call.

CHAPTER 6

Child Mental Health: Marietta Corinelli

Agency:
Children's Mental Health Center, in Cameronsville (pop. 120,000).

Referral date:
October 24, 19xx.

Referral source:
Self, Marietta Corinelli, by phone.

Family data:
Mother: Marietta Corinelli, age 19, born September 19, 19xx.
Child: Michael Corinelli, age 2 1/2, born April 3, 19xx.

Intake interview:
November 7, 19xx.

Phone Conversation

On the phone, Ms. Corinelli said she wanted to talk about a "problem with my son," adding that the pediatrician had recommended that it "was a case for you people." Her son was two and a half years old and she was having "some problems with him, because he seems backward for his age."

Presenting Problem

Marietta requests that we find a permanent residential facility for Michael, who at nearly two and a half years cannot sit alone, doesn't talk, cannot hold a spoon or feed himself, and is not toilet trained.

Marietta told me she had been to "several specialists," all of whom have told her that Michael should be in "a special home for kids like this" because he could "never be looked after in an ordinary family." When I asked her if she had looked into what might be available at the Association for the Developmentally Disabled, she rather angrily rejected this, since she knows "they don't have anything in their school for kids as bad as Michael."

Marietta is a well-groomed young woman, about 5'5", with long dark brown hair loosely teased out around her face and shoulders. She is fine-featured with a light olive complexion and dark brown eyes. She wore a baggy yellow sweater over a white t-shirt and jeans. Michael was not with her at this interview. She told me her mother was looking after him, because "you can't take him on the bus or anything" and her dad has the car at work. I noticed that she chewed gum throughout the interview, and that, sitting with her legs crossed, the free foot swung up and down continually. Her manner was some-what aggressive and at times a little sarcastic. For example, she referred to me as being one of "you people with degrees and all that stuff" who are supposed to know what "kids like Michael really need."

Background Information

Marietta was not quite seventeen when she became pregnant. "I suppose that shocks you." I smiled and said, "No, it doesn't." Marietta said, laughing ruefully, "Well, it sure shocked my parents." Her parents felt disgraced in the close-knit Italian community where they lived. Devout Catholics, they were appalled when the parents of the baby's father not only concurred with their son's refusal to marry Marietta, but even suggested an abortion. The father, Rick, was from a Protestant family. He was seventeen at the time and a bright student in his last year of high school. He is now away at college.

While Marietta spoke in a flip way about this, I noticed that at times she was close to crying. As far as Rick was concerned, she said, "I was good enough to f——, but not to marry, you know the type? Well, no, I guess you wouldn't." She managed to make this sound like a put-down.

Arrangements were made for Marietta to go to an aunt's in another city, to have the baby and give it up for adoption through the child welfare authority there.

Marietta said she pretended to agree to this, but was really determined to keep her baby, because "I always liked little kids, you know?" She thought that if she brought it home her mother would relent and let her stay home and bring up the baby. "Blood's thicker than water, you know?" and also, "Grandmas are real softies, every-one knows that."

While appearing to go along with her parents' plan, a few weeks before she was to give birth she phoned a girlfriend in Cameronsville who was a few years older than she. This girlfriend was separated from her husband and had a one year-old baby. The girlfriend, Joanne, readily agreed to having Marietta come and live with her. It would help them both, she reasoned, since Joanne would be able to work full-time as a waitress while Marietta could collect social assistance, stay home, and look after both children.

Marietta painted a rather pathetic dream picture she had had of herself caring for both children; taking them to the park, having people stop to admire them on the street, and so on. She intended to have them "dressed real cute all the time."

These plans were carried out. However, the living arrangements with Joanne didn't last very long. Marietta got fed up with "just being a nursemaid to Joanne's kid," who was apparently quite active and "a real pain." Also, Joanne went out on dates and left Marietta to babysit, even on weekends. Marietta said she felt like a "slave" and that "it nearly drove me mad just feeding and changing the kids and never seeing anyone to talk to." After about three months they had a major fight, and Joanne "more or less put me out on the street." Marietta said she was glad, really, because "it had been a lot of work, I mean the washing and everything," and Joanne just "lying around the house doing her nails and talking about her boyfriends."

At this point her parents, who had not approved of the plan with Joanne, relented and took her and Michael, then three months old, to live at home. Although Marietta's father still behaved towards her with disapproval, in many ways she found it much easier at home. Her mother helped with Michael, and the family found unexpected support from friends and extended family in the area where they lived.

Michael's development in the next six months seemed very slow, and although Marietta and her mother were not worried, their family doctor suggested they should have the Public Health nurse call. How-ever, neither Marietta nor her parents could accept the nurse's con-cern, and completely rejected her suggestion that the child could benefit from the Infant Development Program at the local hospital. "We thought she was making a big thing out of it because kids don't all grow at the same rate, you know?" An aunt had said there was nothing to worry about, some kids were slower than others.

At the present time, however, Marietta appears determined to find an institutional placement for Michael, and she told me that her mother and her aunt (the one referred to in the previous paragraph), are quite sure that this is the best thing for a child with "this kind of sickness."

CHAPTER 7

Juvenile Probation: Lalanne Dewar

Agency:

Probation Service, Youth Services Division, in Cameronsville (pop. 120,000).

Referral date:

November 30, 19xx.

Referral source:

Probation Intake Division, acting on order of the court.[1]

Personal data:

Lalanne Dewar, age 18, born October 20, 19xx.

Terms of probation:

1. Report every two weeks;
2. Accept counseling re: employment and life-style;
3. Accept counseling re: drug abuse.

First Interview: December 4, 19xx.

Lalanne's appearance is very striking. She is tall, about 5'9", and very slim. She has intense blue eyes and a fair complexion with very fine features. I would call her beautiful. On this occasion she was very heavily made up, and wore a T-shirt, a black leather jacket with fringed trim, and very tight jeans which accentuated her long, slim legs. On entering my office she removed the baseball cap she had been wearing

---

1. The Division serves primarily sixteen and seventeen year-old offenders. Some clients may be older, having committed an offense under age eighteen, but not coming to trial or disposition for some months, due to court backlogs.

to reveal that she had completely shaved her head. She was smoking and chain-smoked throughout the interview.

Throughout the interview she sat eyeing me slightly sideways with an air of exasperated resignation. She volunteered nothing and gave, for the most part, monosyllabic answers to my questions. When she spoke, she scarcely moved her lips, and spoke in such a tiny voice that I often had to ask her to repeat herself.

Lalanne admitted that she is using drugs, "Not the hard stuff," but says she could quit any time "if I felt like it."

As I laid out for her the terms of her probation order, she shrugged her shoulders but said nothing. The only sign of interest she gave was when I raised the question of where she was living and whether or not it was a good idea for her to continue there. If I had met her parents, she said, I would see that her mother was "an old drunk," and her dad was "a wimp." She is presently sharing an apartment with three other girls, one of whom is the sister of the youth with whom she had committed the crimes which had brought her to this agency.

Background

This material is from the presentence report filed with the court, at its request, by J. Killick, Probation Officer, Pre-sentence Reporting Division.

School Record

Lalanne was an above-average student in elementary school and in high school for the first two years. In her junior year, her grades dropped markedly and her attendance became irregular, gradually deteriorating until her sixteenth birthday, when, in an angry exchange, she had thrown her books on the floor of the Vice Principal's office and screamed at her, "I quit your f——ing school for good!" The guidance counselor's attempts to involve her parents in discussing Lalanne's difficulties at school had met with no response. Although appointments were made with each parent, neither of them showed up at the appointed time.

Criminal Record

No previous charges. However, she was known to the Police Youth Bureau to be closely associated with a group of young men who were on probation for having committed a number of breaking and entering crimes in the past year to eighteen months. One of these youths told police that Lalanne had "masterminded" two break-ins of which he was accused. She had reportedly known that the homes in question had, between them, portable radios and other easy-to-sell articles. Ryan (the youth in question) could produce no evidence of Lalanne's complicity, however, and when questioned Lalanne laughed it off as nonsensical.

Present Charge

Lalanne and another youth had broken into two homes in the Turner subdivision. In each case, sums of money had been stolen. In addition, a tape recorder had been taken from one house and, from the other, a Walkman and a box of rock music tapes. These items had apparently been sold for cash to buy drugs.

Family Background

Lalanne's mother is said by Lalanne and her father to be an alcoholic. She was somewhat intoxicated at approximately 10:45 A.M. when the Probation Officer visited, by appointment, for the presentence report. The parents separated when Lalanne was fourteen and have since divorced. Following the separation, Lalanne lived with her mother for a few months, then went to live with her father, and remained there for about six months. She then moved into the apartment with the three other girls.

Her father stated that she became "unmanageable," staying out until "all hours of the night." He often wondered where she got her money, of which at times she seemed to have "plenty," but he never asked her after the first time, when she told him it was "none of his god——n business." He said that sometimes she would be very quiet around the house for a few days, and then she would "go berserk" (his phrase) and fly around the place, slamming things down, screaming at him that she knew he hated her and she wished she had never been born. He had thought she was on drugs but didn't like to ask her, because "it might upset her more." She often said it was his fault that her mother drank.

He admits that one day he lost his temper and told her if she didn't like living with him she could get out. She went upstairs "like a bat out of hell," packed her things, called a taxi and left. He felt badly afterwards, and wondered where she was living. He phoned his ex-wife that night, but she had not seen Lalanne or heard from her.

Later, his girlfriend told him that she had seen Lalanne hanging around the benches outside the Old Courthouse shopping mall, with a group of "young punks" in leather jackets and "ragged clothes" smoking and laughing and making a lot of rowdy noise. A couple of the boys had "mohawk" hairstyles, and Lalanne had a "spiked" hairdo.

Mr. Dewar felt badly that Lalanne was in trouble with the law, but said he had tried his best with her. "There is no guiding teenagers today." He said sadly, "She was such a dear little thing when she was little, we used to go to the store together." Mr. Dewar is rather a meek-mannered man, tall, slightly built, clean-shaven and very neatly dressed. His apartment was very tidy and clean.

As noted above, Mrs. Dewar was intoxicated at the time of the home visit by the Probation Officer and appeared to have gotten out of bed to answer the door. Her hair and general appearance—shabby bathrobe and slippers—were disheveled. Mr. Killick reported that she had an unlit cigarette in her hand as she opened the door, and that her hands shook noticeably as she lit it. She had forgotten he was coming "so early," she said. At times she was barely coherent in answering his questions, and always brought the topic around to her own difficulties, including living on welfare, no one to help her, arthritis in her feet and now beginning in her knees, and a daughter who was no help and could be working and living at home to help out. She said that sometimes she goes to the Broadway Tavern for "a few beers, to be sociable" and "once in a while" she takes a drink at home when she's worried about Lalanne, or her arthritis is real bad. She said that her husband and his girlfriend had turned Lalanne against her. Otherwise, she and Lalanne could be quite happy together.

Mrs. Dewar told the Probation Officer that she was forty years old, but she looked much older to him.

PART TWO

FAMILY SERVICES

CHAPTER 8

Battered Wife: Diana Kingstone

Agency:
   A family service center in a medium-sized industrial city (pop. 130,000).

Referral date:
   June 16, 19xx.

Referral source:
   Ms. L. Marten, Welfare Assistance Worker.

Family data:
   Parents: Don Kingstone, age 38.
   Diana Kingstone, age 27.
   Children: Don, Jr., age 11, born March 1, 19xx.
   Christie, age 10, born April 4, 19xx.
   David, age 7, born December 18, 19xx.

Intake Interview: June 22, 19xx

Ms. Marten is Mrs. Kingstone's welfare worker. She felt that Diana was very depressed, and needed counseling. Her husband left the family the day after Christmas Day, and Diana has been on social assistance since January. Ms. Marten has become increasingly concerned about this client. She is lethargic and has told Ms. Marten that she often goes back to bed after the children have gone to school "just to rest and forget everything." Sometimes she is still asleep when the children come home for their lunch, but she tells Ms. Marten that "young Don is a real help" at such times.

Diana was aware of, and readily agreed, to the referral. We set up an appointment for June 22, 19xx.

Diana presented as a very thin, pale woman, with sharp features and very dark circles under her eyes. She yawned frequently during the interview. Her light brown hair was long—well below her shoulders—and although it looked clean and brushed, it was unstyled and hung over her face.

She was dressed in a dark brown blouse, drab grey sweater and denim skirt, and although her clothes were clean and neat, the overall impression she gave was one of little care or pride in her appearance.

Presenting Problem

Diana's husband, Don, left the family the day after Christmas last year. The day he left he gave her one hundred dollars but has not given her anything since.

The welfare people want her to take some action against Don for support, but she feels she cannot do this, as he finds it so difficult to hold a job, and he "hardly has enough to manage for himself." She has heard that the Welfare Department may take action themselves on her behalf, but she is hoping very much that they won't do this, as it would only turn Don against her and make it unlikely that he will come back to her.[1]

Background Information

Diana was sixteen and a half years of age and four months pregnant when they married eleven years ago. She had been doing well in her junior year of high school but, "Of course I had to quit."

She described Don as a "heavy drinker," and stated that he often beat her while they were together, but only when he was drunk and she "upset him by doing something wrong." This started very soon after they were married, but Diana never considered leaving Don, or bringing any charges, because he did support the family and, "It wasn't as if he ever knocked out any teeth, or broke any bones or anything." She really believes that if only she could have been a better wife and not done things that "upset" Don, things would have been just fine between them. She very much wanted me to understand that he wasn't a "violent" man. He just had trouble controlling his temper when he was drunk and she "upset" him.

1. Some jurisdictions require legal action to be taken against nonsupporting fathers.

Although Don had worked steadily at Howell's Steel in the machine shop for the first five years after they were married, he quit there because a friend told him he was "on to a good thing" in the used car business, and he thought he could make a lot of money if he went in with his friend. This didn't work out, and for the past five years Don has had difficulty finding and keeping steady work. It has been hard to manage on the money he brought home, and Diana feels that her inability to make ends meet was a constant source of aggravation for Don. "If only I'd been smarter with the money, things would have been better," she said. Diana had considered going to work outside the home, but Don had been strongly opposed to this, as he believes that a woman's place is "in the home, caring for her husband and family."

With no marketable skills, Diana has been on welfare since Don left. Two months ago she got into a more reasonably priced, two-bedroom apartment in subsidized housing, and although it is a bit crowded, she finds it easier to manage on the welfare check now.

In reply to my question, she said she used to want to go back to school, but now she does not want to do that, as she believes that this would turn Don against her, and he would not come back to her. She is sure that before long he will get over his affair with "that barfly who took him away from our happy family" and he will come back home "where he belongs." She still loves Don, misses him a lot, and cannot understand what it was she did that made him "up and leave." She did try hard to be the kind of wife and mother Don wanted, and tried every way she knew to please him, but she feels she disappointed him in a lot of ways, and was not always a "good enough" wife for him.

Asked to give an example of this, she remembers that not long before he left, he was late for supper and she didn't know when he would be home. She had put his dinner on a plate in the oven, but had not covered the plate with foil. When Don came home three and a half hours later, his dinner was all dried up. He had been drinking and he shook her and beat her about the face and shoulders. "I should have thought to cover it with foil when he didn't come in after half an hour," she explained. It was her "dumbness" that had "upset him so."

CHAPTER 9

Battered Wife: Katrina Newman

Agency:
"Renata's," a safe house for battered women and their children, in Lakesford, a medium-sized industrial city (pop. 150,000).

Referral date:
April 15, 19xx.

Referral source:
Self, Mrs. Newman, by phone.

Family data:
    Client: Katrina Newman, age 30, born January 14, 19xx.
    Husband: Howard Newman, age 37, born October 26, 19xx.
    Children: Dianne (Dee-Dee), age 11, born December 4, 19xx.
            Jody, age 8, born February 16, 19xx.

Presenting Problem

Mr. and Mrs. Newman have been married for twelve years. The first beatings occurred after the first year of the marriage, and have continued with varying severity ever since. He began to beat the children as "discipline" with his belt and his fists almost as soon as they could run about and get into mischief.

Three days ago, Howard had beaten Dee-Dee with his fists and his belt and had locked her in her bedroom to punish her for talking back to him. Mrs. Newman had threatened to call the child protection services, and he had said, "Go ahead. Who do you think they will believe, you or me?" His challenge frightened her, since his appearance and demeanor was always that of the responsible breadwinner and devoted father and husband. She felt it would be impossible to convince anyone that he was something other than the way he presented himself. However, after this incident, Dee-Dee had threatened her mother she was going to leave home.

Mrs. Newman had made a note of our number when she saw it about two months ago on a bulletin board at the supermarket, and, telling Howard she and the girls were going to visit their maternal grandparents for the weekend, she had phoned us and arrived here by taxi the previous evening.

Background Information

Katrina, now thirty, was eighteen when she married Howard, seven years older than her. Katrina had two sisters older than her, and a younger brother. Dianne, her next older sister, was one year old when Katrina was born. Her mother often told her that she had "hardly recovered" from Dianne's birth when she became pregnant with Katrina. Apparently, Katrina's birth had been difficult for her mother, with a long labor and forceps delivery. Katrina says she always felt to blame for this.

She thinks she was about five or six when her mother complained of feeling ill one day. Katrina had tried to say she was sorry for being such a "bad baby getting born." She remembers that her mother snapped at her that it was too late to say she was sorry now.

Katrina grew up feeling rejected by both parents. She was always forced to give in to her little brother Michael, who was the apple of everyone's eye. Her dad favored the two older girls and of course Michael, but he always used to call her "Kat the Brat" and she felt he always joined her mother in blaming her for things that she knew were the other children's doing.

She has a very dim and confused recollection of her father's brother trying to get her to play with his penis. He used to babysit the two youngest children, and she recalls knowing that there was no one else there with her and Michael. She thinks it happened more than once. Once she thinks she must have screamed or somehow attracted Michael's attention, because she remembers her uncle swearing at Michael when he toddled into the room. He gave her and Michael lots of cookies and said her father would certainly beat her if she told him or her mother anything about it.

She met Howard at her eldest sister's wedding. He was a friend of the groom's family. They began dating soon after the wedding. He was handsome, a good dancer, and co-owner of a very successful travel agency. He had graduated from college with a degree in business, and seemed to her, "a dream husband" in every way. Her parents thoroughly approved, although her Dad often said he couldn't see what a smart guy like Howard could see in her.

She says she was very much in love with him, and was determined to make him a good wife, and prove to him and her family that she was a "good person." She also admitted that marriage was a way to get away from home.

They had been married about a year when Howard first hit her really hard. Before that there had been fights when he had slapped her face a few times, but on this occasion he had held her by one shoulder and really punched her in the face several times.

Later he said he was sorry, and brought her flowers and assured her that it would never happen again. She had had to take a couple of days off work because her eye was blackened and her face bruised and swollen. She believed his excuse that he had a "short fuse" and that she must remember that, and try harder not to get him mad.

From then on things went from bad to worse. When she was pregnant the first time he threw her to the floor and kicked her so fiercely that she miscarried. He refused to take her to the hospital and she felt too sick and frightened to go alone, so she dealt with it herself. She was two months pregnant at the time.

Katrina thought that when the children were born Howard might change, because he had said he wanted children—"A family isn't a family without children." But he was disappointed that they didn't have a son, and blamed her for not being "a *real* woman." A year after Jody's birth she had to have a complete hysterectomy, caused in part, the gynecologist had told her, "by an earlier injury—perhaps a miscarriage?" She had told him of the miscarriage but simply said that it had happened at home early in the pregnancy and he hadn't asked her any more about it. Howard was furious about the hysterectomy and blamed her for not being "woman enough" to give him a son, and also for talking the doctors into doing it to avoid being "a *real* wife." She felt guilty about the hysterectomy and although inwardly relieved that she could not have any more children, this also made her feel guilty because she felt it was both "unwomanly" and against her Catholic upbringing.

The beatings continued and Howard also began to discipline the children with his belt and fists (as noted above). She protected them from him as much as she could, often taking the blame for things they had done: untidiness, eating the last of the muffins, and so forth, but it wasn't always possible. She was so deathly afraid of Howard that she could never bring herself to call the child protection services.

She says it was about the time that Jody started school that she began to consider how she could get away with the girls. She had finished high school before her marriage but had no marketable skills. Howard had twice threatened her that if she left him, he would come after her and kill her and the girls and would make it look like an accident so no one could "pin it on him." She was too afraid of him by then to consider he might be bluffing, and she believed that he was capable of doing this.

Next day, while he was at work, she called the social services anonymously, and asked about a recent article in the local paper about a safe house for battered women and their children. When the woman answering the phone asked if she was inquiring for herself, she hung up, afraid to get into something for which she wasn't truly ready. She was still too frightened of Howard's rage to take any definite steps at that time.

The incident with Dee-Dee and her (Dee-Dee's) subsequent threat to leave home, had finally compelled Katrina to take action, after talking it over with both girls.

Katrina told Howard that she and the girls would go to Townsville to visit their grandparents for the coming weekend. Fortunately, Howard told her he had a business trip arranged for the weekend himself. Katrina saw it as her one and only chance, and she packed up their things as if for a brief visit, phoned us and learned that she could come here immediately. They arrived last evening.

CHAPTER 10

Blended Family:
The D'Angelo Family

Agency:
Family Service Center in a medium-sized city (pop. 125,000).

Referral date:
October 25, 19xx.

Referral source:
Self, Mr. D'Angelo, by phone.

Family data:
Father: Antonio (Tony) D'Angelo, age 41, born 19xx.
Mother: Selma (Giulietto) D'Angelo, age 36, born 19xx.
Children of Mr. D'Angelo's first marriage:
Mariana, age 16, born February 18, 19xx.
Paul, age 13, born July 15, 19xx.
Tony, age 10, born January 4, 19xx.
Child of Mrs. D'Angelo's first marriage:
Benedetta, age 14, born April 16, 19xx.

Note: Antonio and Selma were married four months ago, July 1, 19xx.

Intake interview:
November 2, 19xx.

Presenting Problem

I met with Mr. and Mrs. D'Angelo on November 2, 19xx. They are very concerned about Mariana's behavior and her attitude, which is upsetting the whole family. She is sullen and uncooperative all the time, will not do her share of the housework, in which all the children are supposed to share, and puts Mrs. D'Angelo down continually. For example, Mariana insults her cooking, her accent (Selma came from Italy four years ago), her figure (Selma is about 5'3" and somewhat overweight), her clothes, her hairstyle, and use of make-up. She is sometimes very unkind to Benedetta, her stepsister, in the same ways as towards her stepmother, then suddenly she will be very friendly with the girl, and gives Benedetta the feeling they can be "sisters." Then, just as suddenly, with no apparent reason, she will attack and ridicule Benedetta, often reducing her to tears. It has recently reached a point where Benedetta has threatened to run away.

When Mrs. D'Angelo tries to talk with Mariana about this, the girl often responds with, "I didn't ask for a stepmother, did I?" Mr. D'Angelo implores his wife to overlook the girl's behavior, as she "is having a hard time adjusting." It hurts Mrs. D'Angelo that her husband never rebukes Mariana for her unkindness and lack of consideration towards herself or Benedetta. He just begs Selma to accept that Mariana is "just an unhappy child, after all."

When the boys cooperate with Selma and are friendly with Benedetta, Mariana turns on them and calls them "sucks" and reminds them, "I'm your sister, not her!" Lately they have begun to stand up to her about this, and to defend Selma and Benedetta, which leads to fierce arguments. Selma describes how "everybody is shouting and screaming and slamming doors all over the house."

Selma says she realizes that she cannot take their mother's place with her husband's children, and would like to be a "big sister" to Mariana, but "she hates me, and I cannot get to her, she will not let me." When Selma further said, "I don't know if I can stand to stay," I noted that Mr. D'Angelo's eyes filled with tears, and he put out his hand as if to stop her physically.

Observations

Mrs. D'Angelo was becomingly but very plainly dressed, not stylish, and she wore no make-up. Mr. D'Angelo is about 5'10", thin featured, very well-groomed and neatly dressed in a sportshirt, grey pullover sweater and grey pants. I noticed that his shoes were brightly shined. Selma did most of the talking during the first part of this interview. My attempts to draw him into the discussion met with very brief answers. He would always look at Selma before, and often while, replying. At times while Selma was talking, he hunched over in his chair, and clasped his hands between his knees. At these times, I felt he was near tears.

In response to my comment, "This is a really tough spot for you, isn't it", he replied that he felt "torn in two." He is afraid of losing Selma, yet he feels they must "give Mariana time." He hopes I can "find out what would make Mariana happy."

Background Information

Mr. D'Angelo's first wife died of cancer four years ago. His younger sister lived with them and looked after the children for almost a year, but she found it too demanding. There were some problems with Mariana and with Tony, the youngest boy, and she left.

Mr. D'Angelo and Mariana from then on ran the home "as a team," he said, and things worked out quite well for about two years or so. Then, last May, he met Selma and they started dating. He did not tell the children until he and Selma both felt they were serious about their relationship.

At that point Mariana became very upset, but things really came to a head the first time he invited Selma to the family home for dinner. After dinner he was planning to take Selma to a movie. Mariana had remained in her room while he and the boys cooked dinner. Though she ate with them, she said hardly anything. However, after everything was cleaned up and her father and Selma were getting ready to leave, Mariana went "into hysterics," screaming and shouting that nobody loved her and she would kill herself, and would "find" her mom, and so forth. Both her father and Selma were in great distress. Selma agreed to leave, and the movie plan was cancelled for that night. The next time such an evening was planned, Mariana became sick halfway through dinner, was nauseated, and ran a fever. Again, Selma left and Mr. D'Angelo did what he could to take care of Mariana.

I learned that they had been called back from their very brief (a long weekend) honeymoon because Mariana had been admitted to hospital with severe abdominal pain and nausea. At first thought to be appendicitis, it was diagnosed as being of unknown cause. Only Mr. D'Angelo visited her in hospital. He decided not to bring Selma, for fear of upsetting the girl.

In response to my question, I learned that the children had spent the long weekend of the honeymoon with their mother's older sister, who initially had tried to dissuade Mr. D'Angelo from considering remarriage. This aunt had been very helpful to Mr. D'Angelo and Mariana when they were managing on their own, with tips about cooking, care of clothes, routines, etc.

I told Mr. and Mrs. D'Angelo that I certainly understood that blending two families was by no means an easy task, and they were not alone in having a struggle to make it work. Our agency would certainly help them with their difficulties, but I would not be the worker who would be providing the service. Another worker would be taking over.

I explained that while each of us took our turn taking first calls, we consulted together each week to determine which of us had space in our list to take on a new client family at the earliest possible date. Unfortunately my workload would not allow me to see them for at least six weeks, whereas another colleague would probably see them much sooner than that, probably the week after next. I felt it was important from their point of view that they get started as soon as possible. I would explain to my colleague what they had told me—it would not mean they had to start all over again.

I explained also that the whole family would be expected to come to the sessions together. Mr. and Mrs. D'Angelo seemed very surprised at this. Mr. D. said he couldn't see any point in that. The problem was between Mariana and his wife. They were the ones who needed the help.

I told them that when people come with a family problem this was the way that we offered the service. They would have to decide themselves whether or not they would come as a family, but we would not consider seeing just two members of a family when clearly all family members were being hurt by what was happening.

Mr. D'Angelo said, "Then we all come together or we don't get any help. Is that it?" I said yes, that was the agency's policy.

Mrs. D'Angelo looked at him almost beseechingly, I thought, and he said "We've got no choice—we'll have to try it your way." I said that as soon as I knew the name of their worker and a date when he or she could see them, I would call them to let them know.

CHAPTER 11

Teenage Suicide Attempt: The Dolbeck Family

Agency:
   Crisis Service Unit of a family service agency located in a medium-sized city (pop. 135,000).

Referral date:
   May 14, 19xx.

Referral source:
   Ms. Patricia Andrews, crisis worker. Social Services Department, General Hospital.

Family data:
   Father: Martin Dolbeck, age 40, born April 16, 19xx.
   Mother: Helen Dolbeck, age 42, born December 12, 19xx.
   Children: Karen, age 15, born May 17, 19xx.
                Jonathan, age 12, born March 4, 19xx.
                Jason, age 8, born March 16, 19xx.

Background of the Referral

Karen was admitted to the General Hospital emergency room at 1:00 a.m. May 13th. She had been found by her parents, apparently unconscious, when they returned from a social gathering of business associates at approximately 12:45 a.m. When they could not rouse her, they immediately called an ambulance and Karen was rushed to the hospital emergency room.

The girl was not deeply unconscious, but rather in a condition of heavy stupor. When she came around, she told the nurse that she had taken about half a bottle of aspirin and "about five" tranquilizers she had found in her mother's bedside table, with "a couple of shots" of whiskey with cola. (These quantities were later confirmed by her parents.) Ms. Andrews was the crisis worker on call in social services, and Karen was referred to her by Dr. T. Brodski, physician on duty.

Interview with Karen, May 13, 7:30 a.m., as reported by Ms. Andrews

Karen told Ms. Andrews that she had just felt that "nothing was any use anymore," and that her family would be "better off with her out of the way." Pressed to be more specific, she said that she was failing her year at school and believed that her parents were ashamed of her, because "people in our family just don't fail." She went on to say that things in her family would be perfect if it weren't for her and Jason, they were the "weak ones, especially me." This upsets her parents and then "they fight about things."

When asked for more detail, she described a nightly routine, insisted upon by her mother, where both parents help her and Jason with their homework. Her father resents these demands on his evening leisure time, and often says that mother "overdoes the homework thing." It is his view that if the kids don't want to work they will have to find out for themselves whether good grades are "worth working for." Karen thinks her mother resents the evening routine as well but feels obligated to do something in the face of "her and Jason's laziness."

These fights between her parents are "all my fault. Poor little Jay really tries," she said.

Ms. Andrews had tried to reassure Karen that these things were never any one person's fault, and explained to her that people in families sometimes hurt each other without meaning to, because they were trying to make things better but didn't know how.

Ms. Andrews had explained to Karen that she believed her family could be helped and that she was going to recommend to her parents that they should get family counseling. She told Karen how family therapists work and how research showed that seeing the whole family together was the best way to help. Karen did not think her parents would consent to this. Ms. Andrews said she would talk to them about it and recommend it when she saw them later in the morning when they came to take Karen home.

In her brief interview with Mr. and Mrs. Dolbeck, Ms. Andrews had found them both very shaken by Karen's suicide attempt, and both had expressed that they had had no idea that she felt so depressed by her failure at school. Mrs. Dolbeck, in particular, had seemed very frightened that their methods of dealing with the children might be at fault. Mr. Dolbeck had appeared "bewildered and overwhelmed," and said very little.

Ms. Andrews had strongly recommended that they get family counseling from our agency and requested their permission to make the referral. At first both were quite hesitant about such a plan. Ms. Andrews had said she could see that Karen's suicide attempt had been a shock to them and believed that they and Karen needed professional help in working this out together. In addition, she gave them a detailed explanation of the family therapy process, reassuring them that it did not mean they were being "judged" about their parenting. She described our agency and said she would make the referral to our crisis unit, so that they could be seen as soon as possible. They agreed to the referral, and Ms. Andrews recommended that they tell Karen and the boys about this plan.

Karen was released to them immediately following this interview.

Intake Phone Call to Family: May 16th

When I phoned the Dolbecks to introduce myself and offer them an appointment for the next day, Mrs. Dolbeck suggested that it might be better to wait a while, to "let things simmer down a bit" before they came to see me. I said I didn't think that was really very wise.

Recognizing that the idea of family therapy was very new to them, and that I was yet another stranger to talk to about their concerns, I said that I believed that their taking immediate action on this would, in the first place, reassure Karen of their concern. I said I also believed that they would actually find it easier to start work now, rather than to put it off, wondering what it was going to be like and not getting any help in handling their own feelings and the children's questions.

Mrs. Dolbeck excused herself to speak to her husband. She came back and said yes, they would start whenever I could see them, but asked "if the boys really have to come too" as she and her husband felt it would upset their routines and worry them. I explained that I would like to see her and her husband alone this first time, but that it was very important for the boys to know that they were to be included. It was important that everyone in the family was involved in talking about what was hurting in the family, how they felt about it, and what they could do together to make things better. Everyone needed to hear what was said. Mrs. Dolbeck replied, rather doubtfully I thought, "Yes, I see."

We made an appointment for Friday, May 17.

Interview with Mr. and Mrs. Dolbeck: May 17th

Both parents presented a very well-dressed, well-groomed appearance, but appeared very ill-at-ease as they entered my office. I noticed that they sat markedly far apart on the couch. Mrs. Dolbeck said immediately that they were completely at a loss as to why Karen would do anything like this. "We've tried so hard to be good parents," she said, near to tears. Mr. Dolbeck looked out the window and said, almost as if to himself, "Maybe we've tried too hard." Mrs. Dolbeck looked quickly at him and then back to me and said, "You do what you think is right for them, but God knows if . . ." and she trailed off, beginning to cry.

I said I could understand that this had been a very frightening experience for them, but Karen was alive and I understood she was physically OK, and we were here to help them all look together at what was hurting the family so much that she had tried to take her own life. Mrs. Dolbeck asked what I meant by something "hurting the family." She said she felt "something was hurting Karen." I said that in my experience when one member of a family is hurting, the whole family is troubled. Healing comes about when all family members are involved, together, in looking at what is happening, their feelings about it, and what can be done to change things for the better. Mrs. Dolbeck began to cry again, and said she "felt so ashamed," adding that surely Karen didn't need to "bring this on us all."

Mr. Dolbeck said he had read an article about family therapy in the local newspaper, but thought it was just used with alcoholic families or where parents "didn't get along." I explained it had been found to be the most effective way of helping families with all kinds of struggles that were getting in the way of their being happy together. "But she tried to kill herself," he said, shaking his head, and added, "We should have taken it more seriously the last time." Mrs. Dolbeck looked sharply at him again and said quickly that he had "agreed" at the time that to "give in" to Karen wouldn't have been "constructive," adding to me that they had felt that with a thirteen-year-old, "You just don't fall for every little whim."

Mr. Dolbeck looked miserably out of the window again and said, "It was against my better judgment." Mrs. Dolbeck looked at him, almost beseechingly, I thought, and said, "I don't think it's all my fault."

I said these things are never all one person's "fault," and in any event, the purpose of family therapy was not fault-finding or blame-placing. That was a complete waste of time. They would be helped to look at what was happening in the family, how each one felt about it, and what, together, they could do to change things.

In reply to my question about their reference to "the last time," I learned that Karen had made two previous "gestures" (Mrs. Dolbeck's phrase). When she was eleven, she made several cuts on one wrist with a jacknife. Mrs. Dolbeck said they were quite shallow cuts on her forearm, well above the wrist and easily dealt with at home. She had told Karen her actions were dangerous, but had felt the girl was "dramatizing" her failure to come first in a city-wide essay contest. (She had received "honorable mention.") Mrs. Dolbeck said they had both felt that if they just ignored the behavior—"It seemed to us it was just a bid for attention"—Karen would forget all about it. They had encouraged her to enter the essay contest again, and to "try harder the next time."

The second "gesture" was when Karen was thirteen. She had virtually stopped eating for almost three days, drinking only water and a glass of juice at mealtimes, saying she wasn't hungry. She had told them she wished she was dead, but would not tell them why. They gave up trying to get her to eat, and "just ignored it," but when she had fainted at school, they had become alarmed and on the advice of the school nurse took her to their pediatrician. She advised that Karen should stay out of school for a week, eat normally, remain in the house, and "do things that she really likes to do."

Mrs. Dolbeck said that at the time they had a daily housekeeper of whom the children were very fond. They found that Mrs. Bertulli was "coddling" Karen, spending a lot of time with her and making her specially tempting and favorite foods, and they didn't approve of this. They believed that Karen would learn that she could get favored status and attention if she "pulled these stunts," and that this was not good for her. Mrs. Dolbeck said they had "put a stop to this." They insisted that Karen do school work at least two hours each day, which one of her parents would review with her in the evening. She was also to help the housekeeper with household chores in the mornings, these to be recorded for their information each day. Mrs. Dolbeck said pleadingly, "I honestly, I mean, we honestly thought that was the right thing to do." She added that it is "such a shock to think you may have been doing it wrong all the time," and she began to cry again. Mr. Dolbeck moved closer to her on the couch and took her hand. "We both need help," he said.

Mrs. Dolbeck said that Ms. Andrews' calling this latest incident "a crisis" had frightened her. Did I really think they needed "crisis service?" I responded that our service was called this because we found it was important for families to get help as soon as possible after such an event. I added that what was positive about it was that such a critical event was often the turning point for a family in setting their life on a different, more rewarding, and happier path.

I asked about the other children, and learned that Jonathan is "absolutely no problem at all." He is very good at mathematics and science, is at the top of his class, and regularly comes first in city-wide contests. Most recently he had won a state-wide math contest for junior high pupils.

Jason, who is eight years old, is having some health problems. He doesn't sleep well, and Mrs. Dolbeck said he had recently been diagnosed as having an ulcer. They were surprised because he has always seemed a very quiet, "contented" child. He likes baseball and "tries hard" to play well. He is trying to become good enough to get on a little league team next year. Presently, he plays in the elementary school orchestra, playing violin, for which he takes private lessons. He does "only fairly well" at school, and they recently suggested to his teacher that he be given extra homework which they could help him with at night and on weekends. The teacher had suggested in January that Jay should be seen by the school psychologist, but they had vetoed this as "ridiculous," feeling there was nothing "mentally wrong with him." She (the teacher) had not been in favor of the extra homework plan, but they had insisted, Mrs. Dolbeck said, feeling that she was being "too easy" on Jason. However, their pediatrician has recommended that they drop this for a while, because of the ulcer, but they remain concerned that he will "fall behind" in his grades.

Jason is very close to Karen, and both parents expressed concern that she is "not a good example" for him in connection with school work. They worry about how Jason will react to this present incident with Karen. Mrs. Dolbeck looked at me and said they had been feeling that the less said about it to the boys, the better. Did I think that was best? I said I had found that it was always best to give children the opportunity to talk about their fears, and that I thought they would be wise to talk it over with the boys, reassure them about Karen's recovery, and make sure that they understood why they would be included in the family therapy work.

I noticed that in this interview Mrs. Dolbeck did most of the talking. When I returned to Mr. Dolbeck he said, rather timidly, I thought, that Karen's overdose had "frightened" him. He wondered if she was really that afraid of failing at school. She had always seemed to him a "bright little thing," but from third grade on, her grades had been very disappointing. He had often kidded her about having to pull up her socks if she was going to "follow in Dad's footsteps" and become an engineer. Perhaps she didn't want to do that, he said, almost seeming to question me on this. Perhaps she would rather teach history, like her grandmother.

Family Background

Father is a senior chemical engineer with Halversen Paper Company. Mother is a C.P.A. with a prestigious local firm, affiliated with a national corporate conglomerate. Grandparents on both sides were college graduates. Mr. Dolbeck's father is a mining engineer, Mrs. Dolbeck's father is a lawyer. Father's mother teaches history at State University. Mother's mother was a full-time homemaker but was always very active in community work. Since her children grew up, she has served on several local boards where they live, including the hospital, the Board of Education and, currently, the City Council.

We made an appointment for the whole family one week from this date.

CHAPTER 12

Marital Separation: Loretta Lawson

Agency:
Family Service Center, in a medium-sized industrial town (pop. 120,000).

Referral date:
October 18, 19xx.

Referral source:
Self, Mrs. Loretta Lawson, by phone.

Family data:
    Mother: Loretta Lawson, age 40, born March 21, 19xx.
    Children: Leanne, age 14, born February 2, 19xx.
                Jimmy, age 11, born October 5, 19xx.

Intake interview:
November 1, 19xx, with mother alone.

Presenting Problem

Mrs. Lawson left her husband in February of this year because of his heavy drinking. Although she is able to support the children and herself and is receiving some sporadic support payments from her husband, the move has resulted in a marked reduction of living standard for all three of them, and she feels guilty about this for the children's sake. The children resent this, and blame her.

Over the spring and summer the children have become increasingly unruly at home. They refuse to do anything she asks of them. Leanne will not tell her where she is going, or with whom. Jimmy is surly and uncommunicative one minute and yelling obscenities at her the next. Both children's school grades have gone down markedly compared with last year. Mrs. Lawson feels she has completely lost control of the children, and feels "at the end of my rope."

Background Information

Mr. and Mrs. Lawson were married sixteen years ago. She was then twenty-four and he twenty-five. They met in the church choir in her hometown, a small country town about forty miles outside of Mainsville. They dated for about a year and a half before marriage. Loretta described her husband at that time as a "real charmer," good-looking and lots of fun to be with. Occasionally at parties he would have too much to drink, in her view, but he was always very apologetic afterwards, and it never got to the point of his "making a fool of himself." By this she meant that while he would laugh uproariously and "clown around," he never did anything offensive for which he would later have to apologize. He used to tell her, "I might be a little boring when I've had one too many, but you can't say I'm nasty or vulgar," and she had had to admit that was true.

When they married he was selling cars. He was a very good salesman, and regularly was named "salesman of the month" with the firm.

Loretta worked as an executive secretary until Leanne was born, and then stayed home full-time for nearly five years with the children. It was towards the end of this time that she felt Kevin began to be "the first one drunk at every party," but he never drank during working hours, and never missed work because of a hangover. About once a month he would be away all day on a Saturday, telling her he had to "clinch a couple of car deals," but he would come home in the early hours of the morning, by taxi, and she would hear him fumbling at the door with his keys. On these occasions he would sleep, fully clothed, on the couch, "so's not to disturb me." Once she got up and tried to tell him how this behavior was making her feel, and he had yelled at her and told her to leave him alone and to "spare me your sermons!"

In between these episodes he would often be just the same as before, charming and fun, and occasionally would bring her flowers or perfume to surprise her. But the heavy drinking episodes gradually became more frequent. She thinks it was about four years ago that Kevin began drinking after work, would come home late for supper, and yell at her and the kids "for nothing."

From then on until Christmas, two years ago, Kevin's drinking progressed rapidly to serious problem proportions. He lost one job after another, yet was always able to stay sober long enough to establish himself with a new employer (usually in the car business) and was such a good salesman that they made all kinds of concessions to keep him on as long as they could. When she finally refused to phone and make excuses for him to his boss, he became increasingly hostile to her and the children, who retreated into miserable silence when he was home and stayed out of his way as much as possible.

Finally, after a New Year's Eve party at work, at which Kevin got very drunk and vulgarly insulted his boss' wife and another woman employee, he was gone for almost a week and Loretta didn't know where he was. She determined then to leave, and in early February she told Kevin she was going. He had cried at first, and begged her to stay and "help him with his problem," but when he saw she was adamant, he cursed her out and told her it was "good riddance" for him.

She found an apartment in the Maple Hill area, and there was enough furniture in the home to furnish it for herself and the children, still leaving Kevin adequately provided for. She has kept her job at Bowman Industries, where she has worked for nearly seven years, and is able to manage a modest living for the three of them. Kevin had agreed to contribute to the children's support, but she cannot count on it. Financially, "it's tight, but I manage," she said. She feels it is just a matter of time before they will have to sell the house.

Children's Relationship with Father

While it was a relief to the children to be away from the tension, fights, and continual stress of the last two or three years, both have had to change schools and, of course, both miss their friends.

Leanne, who remembers her dad clearly as a warm, fun person when she was little, is particularly vulnerable to his occasional tearful phone calls to her and Jimmy about his loneliness and how much he misses them.

Sometimes he arranges to meet the children, arrives sober, and gives them a great time with dinner at McDonald's and an hour or so at Roller Country. This reinforces their affection and keeps alive their hope he will quit drinking. But his many broken promises—when he is very late, shows up drunk, or just does not show up at all for a planned visit—keep them on edge.

He is often late and unreliable in support payments, and when she must refuse them a treat, it hurts her, but she feels she must "put the blame where it belongs." When she tells them, "If your father would pay up what he owes us . . .," Leanne sometimes yells at her,

"You were the one that left!" Lately, Jimmy just covers up his ears and runs into his room.

Children's Relationship with Mother

Loretta says that when she first moved to Maple Hill, she felt very sorry for the children in their new situation—a two-bedroom apartment in which Leanne must share her mother's bedroom, no yard, sun deck or family room, and so on. She had tried to make it up to them by doing more for them, expecting less of them in household chores, and driving them across town so they could join in activities with their friends in their former area. Now she has begun to feel like "their slave." They do not even say "please" anymore when asking for things at the table.

She would like them to stay home with her in the evenings, but they say that's "too boring" and they want to be with the new friends they have made at school and in the area. They accuse her of "moaning and groaning all the time about everything" and they are sick of listening to her.

Other Information

Loretta has cut herself off from her former social group and all her friends except one very close woman friend, as she has learned that her husband is spreading stories about her dating other men, hanging out in bars, and so on, and feels her only defense is to stay home in the evenings. She feels very much alone in the situation.

I explained to Mrs. Lawson that I would like to see her and the children together, as this has been found to be the most effective method in helping with family difficulties. She wondered if it wouldn't be more helpful if I saw the children alone? I said we would look at that later on, as we got to know each other, and as we all began to understand just what was hurting them all, but certainly at the beginning I would expect them all to come to the sessions. This way everyone hears what is said, everyone feels they have a chance to be heard; and no one is singled out as being either "the problem" or as having sole responsibility for bringing about change for the better.

Mrs. L. said she could see the point in that—it would help to "share the load around." We made an appointment for them for two weeks from today.

PART THREE

ADOPTION COUNSELING

CHAPTER 13

Teenage Pregnancy:
Katharine Westley

Agency:
Family and Children's Services: Unmarried Parents Service, Lakesford (pop. 150,000).

Referral date:
March 15, 19xx.

Referral source:
Katharine Westley, by phone, stating she is 17, and is three months pregnant, wishes to discuss adoption plans.

Family data:
Westley Family
Father: Arthur Westley, age 35.
Mother: Caroline Westley, age 33.
Children: Katharine, age 17, born September 21, 19xx.
Douglas, age 15, born August 14, 19xx.
Robert, age 14, born November 1, 19xx.
Christopher, age 10, born May 16, 19xx.

Koslik Family
Father: Walter Koslik, age 53.
Mother: Maria Koslik, age 50.
Children: Sarah, age 30, R.N., working away from home.
Stephen, age 28, professional engineer, also working away from home.
James (father of the expected child), age 19, born February 2, 19xx, in final year of high school, living at home.

First Interview

Katharine was accompanied to the first interview by her father and mother, James (Jim) Koslik, who admits that he is the father of the expected child, and his parents.

Kathy had told me on the phone that she was pregnant and wished to place the baby for adoption. Greeting her in the waiting room, she introduced me to the others, and I asked if she wished to see me alone, or if she wished the others to be present. Before she could answer, Mr. Koslik, already on his feet, said, "This is a family matter," and Kathy said with noticeable poise, I thought, "It's best if they all come in for now." Mr. Koslik was the first to follow me out of the door and to the interview room.

As we discussed the matter, it became clear that Kathy was under a great deal of pressure from both sets of parents to marry Jim. Both families would help, they said firmly, and see to it that "the kids got off to a good start." In response to my question, they replied that they meant this in both a financial sense and in terms of helping them with the care of the baby when it arrived.

Both young people are still in high school, and Jim had definite plans for college. However, his father said that was now out of the question, and he would get Jim a job in the meatpacking plant where he himself worked. Kathy's mother said Kathy must also give up any "big ideas" she had had about higher education, and stay home and care for the baby.

I noted that in saying this Mrs. Westley smiled broadly. Kathy looked at her mother and said bitterly, "Just like you did?" and her dad said gently and reproachfully, "Now, Kathy. . . ."

Throughout this interview, Mr. Koslik and Mrs. Westley did, markedly, most of the talking. I attempted to draw Jim in, asking him how he felt about what was best for him and Kathy and the baby, but his father answered immediately, "He wants to do the right thing, he's always been a good kid, and he's not going to weasel out of his duty now." Mr. Koslik looked at Jim, and Jim said quietly that he "wanted to do the right thing for Kathy."

I said I knew Kathy was thinking about adoption, as she had told me on the phone, and I was going on to explain the agency's service when Mrs. Westley interrupted with, "That's out of the question," and Mr. Koslik chimed in, "This child is our flesh and blood—it's our first grandchild." I noticed that Mrs. Koslik reached for his hand, and her eyes filled with tears, but he didn't make any move towards her.

Except for the one outburst noted above, Kathy remained very calm and quiet throughout. But her face seemed "set" most of the time, and I thought she looked very determined. She held her head high, and it appeared to me that she felt she was letting the adults speak their piece, biding her time, so to speak, as if this were a tiresome preliminary to her stating her own views.

I explained that the agency would want to help them look carefully at this decision, as it had to be one with which they could all live comfortably for a long time. For everyone's sake, whatever was decided had to be firmly agreed upon, and a firm commitment made by the young people themselves, if there were not to be regrets, perhaps recriminations, down the road. Kathy nodded her head slowly and very definitely at this.

Mrs. Westley said that of course Kathy could remain at home during the pregnancy, but she hoped that the wedding could be soon, and that I would not try to delay things too long. Mr. Koslik said he knew that agencies liked to get young women away into "Homes" during their pregnancy, so that we could work on them to put the baby up for adoption, and thus "please the rich people waiting for a child," but they would care for Kathy themselves until the wedding if her parents had any difficulties about this.

At this, Kathy rolled her eyes and looked in exasperation at the floor.

I commended both families for being supportive of the young people and wanting to be there for them if they decided that marriage was the best thing for them, but I reiterated that I believed that Kathy and Jim had to take the responsibility themselves for making the decision about the baby. I said I understood the families' feelings about its being their grandchild, and could see that this was important to Mr. and Mrs. Koslik, but that my experience had been that often people had serious regrets if the decision—either way—was made too fast.

I then suggested that I would like to see Kathy alone. Mrs. Westley said she thought she had better come along, because Kathy had some "pretty funny ideas," and she (Mrs. Westley) would be better able to explain things for her. At this point, Kathy said very firmly indeed, "Thank you, I'll come on my own." I said if Mrs. Westley would kindly bring Kathy, I would see her first and then Mrs. Westley immediately afterwards.

I then said I would also like to see Jim alone. He looked hesitantly at his father, and Mr. Koslik said he couldn't see much point in that. He reminded me that Jim had already told me he wanted to do the right thing, and that was the beginning and end of it. I agreed that Jim had told me this, and I commended him for it, but I said that, realizing that he and Kathy did not agree at the present time about what was best for them and for the baby, I believed it was important to help Jim think about, and talk about what this disagreement meant to him, and about the future, and his responsibilities, whichever way Kathy eventually decided.

Mr. Koslik said he could already see that I was going to "push" Kathy to give the baby up and I had better think of what my responsibilities were to "the adults in this situation," and that Kathy was still "a child under the law." I said I could understand that it was difficult for him to trust me—we had never met until this morning, and he had heard things he didn't like about workers in agencies such as mine. However, I asked him to try to believe me when I said that my professional ethics were solidly against "pushing" anyone into any decision in such an important matter as this and that I was professionally obligated to help people think very carefully through the decision about what is best for everybody.

Second Interview

Mrs. Westley and Katharine were both in the waiting room when I went out to meet Kathy. Mrs. Westley stood up as if to come with us, but Kathy said to her very emphatically, "Mother, I am seeing her first, you can wait here for *your turn*." This last was given in a very sarcastic tone.

In this interview, Kathy said her mind was completely made up. She wished to get away somewhere as soon as possible, and give up the baby for adoption, for its sake, as well as for hers and Jim's. Her manner was calm and firm but not at all aggressive. She asked me to help her with these plans. I asked her to tell me more about how she had arrived at this decision.

Kathy told me that her own family background has been chaotic. Her mother had become pregnant with Kathy at sixteen; her dad was, at that time, eighteen. "They had to get married," she said. There were two boys younger than her, with barely eighteen months between each of the children. Her mother left the family when Kathy was about five, and was away for almost a year. The children were placed with a farm family they knew, and saw their father about once a month. At that time he worked on freighters on the Great Lakes so they were used to not seeing him for fairly long stretches at a time. They did not see their mother at all during this time. Her mother returned home and the family was reunited. About six months later her mother gave birth to another baby boy, Christopher, who was accepted into the family, but Kathy remembers that from the time

64

shortly after her mother's return, "the fights began. My parents—rather I should say my mother—fought and screamed a lot, but my dad was mostly pretty quiet," because "she out-yells him every time."

From then on, Kathy recalls her mother leaving the home several times, usually taking Christopher with her. These occurred when Kathy was about seven, again when she was nearly ten, and again when she was fourteen years old. During the last separation the children had lived with an uncle and aunt, their father's sister, and had been very happy there. Kathy remembers that one evening her dad had asked his sister if the children's mother could visit them. Her aunt had refused, saying that it would only upset the children, and "What good would it do?" Her aunt also said, "There's no future in it, for them or for you." She admits she was eavesdropping and should not have heard all this. But she heard her aunt telling her dad that he would be crazy to take her back again. Later, she says she remembers hearing her dad crying in the bedroom next to hers. "It was such an awful sound," she said. Kathy said that for some reason the phrase "There's no future in it" has stayed with her.

Kathy said that although she loves her father, she despises him for being such a "wimp" and taking her mother back every time. She added that her aunt and uncle, who are childless, would have kept them until they were grown up. As it is, with all the changes and so on, all three of the children are behind in school, and the boys are beginning to get into trouble with the law. Kathy feels this is because, "We never knew whether we were coming or going as kids."

She cannot respect, or even like, her mother. Lately her mother has tried to say they are "more like sisters," especially when they are with friends or relatives, but Kathy feels this is her mother's attempt to stay young. At times Kathy feels they do have—on good days—a kind of sisterly relationship in that they can sometimes laugh at the same things, and enjoy shopping together. But then her mother switches over to a critical, downgrading way with Kathy, and "it all blows apart again."

Kathy and Jim have been dating for about six months. She does like him a lot, but feels he is completely under his father's thumb, and wishes he was more assertive. He definitely wants to go to college and become a physicist—"He's a real brain"—and she is quite sure he is only going along with the plan for marriage because his father says it is the right thing for him to do. Kathy is frightened that he will hold it against her all their lives that he couldn't pursue the career he both wants and appears to be well suited for.

I asked about her thoughts on a career. She says she knows she could handle college work—her teachers all tell her so—and they have told this to her parents. However, she is a year behind where she should be, and is still two years away from completing secondary school. Her mother continually puts her down about this, saying things like, "Slow learners like you have to be realistic about education." At this, for the first time since I had met her, Kathy's eyes filled with tears. She reached for a tissue and apologized. I said that must hurt her a lot, and she said yes, it did, because if she hadn't had to change schools so often, and been so mixed up all the time, she feels sure she would be further ahead by now, and all this was because her mother deserted the family "every couple of years."

Kathy feels she must get away from the family. She believes that her aunt and uncle, who have now retired to a retirement community about 315 miles away, would have her stay with them during her pregnancy. If everything goes well, and the baby can be placed for adoption in Townsville, where her aunt and uncle live, she could then get a job—any kind of job—and start supporting herself until she can find a way to get back to school and get some professional education. She would really like to become a travel agent.

She thinks I will have a hard time persuading her mother and Mr. Koslik that she is definitely not going to marry Jim, and said she is afraid I might "weaken" because they can be pretty "hardnosed" when they want their own way. I tried to reassure her that I would always keep in the center of my attention my responsibility to help her make the decision she felt was right for her, Jim, and the baby.

As she left, she looked at my degrees on the wall, said she guessed it must have taken a long time to get them, and asked had I enjoyed going to college. I said yes, I had. There were times when I had found it heavy going but it was worth it in the end. She said, "Lucky you," and we shook hands.

CHAPTER 14

Adoption Disclosure:
Maureen Lenham

Agency:
Adoption service in a child welfare agency in Cameronsville (pop. 120,000).

Referral date:
July 27, 19xx.

Referral source:
Self, Ms. Maureen Lenham, by phone.

Personal data:
Maureen Lenham, age 40, born January 23, 19xx.

Ms. Lenham phoned for an appointment on the above date. Her speech was rather slurred and she made several long pauses and occasionally laughed inappropriately while she talked. I thought perhaps she had been drinking. She said she wanted to discuss an adoption "of twenty years ago." When I asked if it was her own adoption, she said, "Well, not exactly," and asked if we could "save the details" (laughing quite loudly) until I could see her. I accepted this and we made an appointment for July 30, 19xx.

First Interview: July 30, 19xx

Note: the receptionist later told me that Ms. Lenham was almost twenty minutes early for her appointment, and that she had expressed humorous relief to learn, in answer to her question, that smoking was permitted in the waiting room. The receptionist, an experienced, mature employee, felt Ms. Lenham had been a little "loud" and inappropriate in her attempts to converse with her and other waiting clients while she waited.

Ms. Lenham is about 5'5" tall and very thin. She looks almost haggard, with very fine features and dark circles under her eyes. She was very plainly dressed in a dark blue skirt and blouse. Both looked slightly worn. Her dark, medium-length straight hair hung around her face apparently without any attempt at styling. In the interviewing room she exclaimed, "Gee, you've got pretty chairs and everything!" I said the interviewing rooms had recently been redecorated and we were happy with our "new look." I said I was glad she liked it. She laughed loudly and said she had thought it would be "more like a jail."

I asked her to tell me about the adoption she had mentioned on the phone, and she said it was a long story and asked if she could smoke. I noticed that her hands shook a little while she lit her cigarette. She chain-smoked throughout the interview.

She told me that on July 27th, eighteen years ago, she had had a baby girl. She was then unmarried, just twenty-two years of age, and had one more semester before graduation from college with a B.A. in economics. She had dropped out of school at Christmas that year but fully intended to return and complete her degree. The baby's father was also at college, intending to pursue a law degree. She laughed loudly and said the baby was "just one of those silly mistakes." It interrupted their lives and neither of them wanted "to settle down with a crying infant on our hands." She laughed loudly again (to me, it seemed forced) as she said this, but the laugh caught in her throat and her eyes filled with tears. I said perhaps it hadn't been quite such an easy decision as she was trying to say it was. She replied that at the time it was easy, but now when she thinks about it, "it's a bit different." She continued, "I couldn't even think up a name for it," adding, "We were just kids, you know?" When she went to sign the adoption consent papers, she learned the nurses at the hospital had named the baby Cheryl.

After graduation she had worked in an investment company until, at age twenty-five, she had married an "up and coming" young man in the same business. "People said we were the ideal couple, goodlooking, ambitious, on the way up." It was all very romantic at first, but, as time went on, things "went sour." Her husband, Ted, was very ambitious, and soon started his own investment business. He worked evenings and on weekends to get ahead. He had little time for her, and gradually they did nothing together other than obligatory social occasions connected with his business. He was, however, a devoted father. His own father had been partially disabled in a work accident and was in a wheelchair from the time Ted was eleven years old. He planned meticulously for regular time with their two children, "as soon as they could talk and were toilet-trained," she said bitterly. He was adamant about her not working outside the home and she began to feel cut off from him as a person, and shut out of his relationship with the children, as well. She felt as if she was his housekeeper, hostess and sex partner, but not his wife. "I was well paid, but it wasn't my life," she told me.

She began to drink "a bit" at home, alone, and after a while her husband "used it as an excuse" to leave her, taking the children to his parents. At the time of the subsequent divorce she had become so upset that, "I was in a bit of trouble with the drinking," and she did not attempt to contest his custody or to ask for visiting rights. She just dropped out of their lives. Immediately following the divorce, she moved up here to Jarvistown to "start anew."

I asked if she had kept in touch with the children—now twelve and fifteen years of age—in any way. She said that "lately" she had been sending them birthday and Christmas cards "from time to time" but not regularly. They had always sent her a Christmas card. This year her fifteen-year-old daughter had sent her a card for Mother's Day—it was quite a surprise—and in it had told her that their father had remarried "a lovely person, and we are all together and very happy now." At this Ms. Lenham began to cry bitterly, and apologizing for "being such a wimp," she sobbed uncontrollably for a while. I said she needn't apologize—I thought she needed to cry.

She said she feels so terribly alone and asked if I knew that song "Sometimes I Feel Like a Motherless Child"? I said yes, and she said that was how she feels most of the time, adding that she knew she shouldn't feel sorry for herself. I said it was OK to feel sorry for the "motherless child" and that perhaps later on we can find a way for her to comfort that child. I asked about her own family.

Her parents both died in a car accident when she was thirteen. She was an only child, and after her parents' death, she was brought up by a kind but very strict uncle and aunt, her father's sister. They had no children themselves. She believes that her father was drunk at the time of the accident, but it was one of those things a child surmises from things people let drop, but never fully discuss. However, her aunt and uncle often warned her against the "evils of alcohol" when she was at school and college. "But, of course, I just went with the crowd."

After she moved up here she "took a couple of runs at AA," and it helped her a lot. She has the drinking under control now. "It never was that serious, really," it was just her unhappiness in her marriage that drove her into it and she didn't need AA anymore. She has worked in a variety of jobs since coming here and now works in retail sales and enjoys it, "but of course I was trained for something more professional."

She has recently seen a couple of programs on TV about adopted people searching out and meeting their birth mothers. Now that the baby she gave up is eighteen years of age, she would like to register with the adoption agency in Cameronsville that she is willing to be contacted if her daughter ever wants to get in touch.

She looked very directly at me with her head on one side and asked in almost a challenging way, "What do you think?"

I said we saw a lot of both young and older people who had been adopted to whom their birth mother's readiness to meet them had meant a great deal. I thought it was very brave of her to consider this, and that I felt it had taken a lot of guts for her to come here to talk about it.

She bridled a bit and asked "Why 'brave'? You make it sound kind of dangerous." I said that in my experience there were certainly some risks on both sides in such a contact, but I believed that by talking about these it would help her to weigh the risks against the advantages for herself and her daughter. Maureen asked me what kind of risks was I talking about. I said, for example, sometimes in their teens an adopted child whose adoption has not been a happy experience blames their birth mother for it, not being old enough to understand their mother's reasons for giving her up. Or, alternatively, perhaps her daughter would never feel the need to contact her and she would need to look at the possibility that she might never know her daughter.

I said it sounded to me like she had never really talked to anyone about the whole experience and that I believed it would help if we talked these things over. She could think things through and it would help her not only to decide if she wanted to go through with register-ing, but also to prepare herself for the contact if it worked out. Maureen looked down at her hands and said nothing for a moment. Then she said, yes, she thought that made sense. We made an appointment for the same day and time next week.

CHAPTER 15

Adoption Disclosure: Mark Lindsay

Agency:
> Adoption service in a child welfare agency in a medium-sized city (pop. 125,000).

Referral date:
> July 31, 19xx.

Referral source:
> Self, Mark Lindsay, by phone.

Personal data:
> Mark Lindsay, age 28, born June 11, 19xx, married, one son, age 7 months.

Mark Lindsay phoned asking for an appointment to discuss the possibility of locating and meeting with his birth father. He already knows his birth mother, who, until the death of his adoptive grandmother in January, he had known as his Aunt Laurie.

He said he would like to come in on his own "at least for the first time," as there were some "complicating factors" that would need talking over before other family members could be involved. We made an appointment for August 4, 19xx.

First Interview: August 4, 19xx

Mark is about 6'2" tall, with very fair complexion, blond hair, regular features, and strikingly blue eyes. He presented a generally well-groomed appearance.

He was adopted as an infant by his birth mother's sister and her husband, who were unable to have children of their own. His adoptive mother was unable to sustain a pregnancy successfully. He had known from an early age that he was adopted, but not that his "Aunt Laurie" was his birth mother. His parents had been very loving. His maternal grandparents also lived here in Jarvistown and he was very much a part of the extended family. He feels he had a very happy childhood. His mother's family are of Finnish descent; his adoptive father had immigrated from Scotland.

His adoptive father died very suddenly of a heart attack when Mark was nine years old. He missed his father dreadfully for a long time. His adoptive mother never remarried. She was always very loving and supportive in all his activities, school and sports, which were an important part of his growing-up years, but he always envied the other guys whose fathers came out to games and so on and cheered their kids on. His maternal grandfather was "more or less an invalid," and died when Mark was thirteen.

In his early teens he had found among some old photos, a picture of one of his maternal uncles as a teenager that looked, to him, strikingly like himself. He had asked his adoptive mother how they had managed to get a child that so much resembled her family. His mother had answered that they had specially asked for a child of Scandinavian background, but he sensed, "as kids do," that she had been upset by such a question. He said he felt that he got "mixed messages" from his adoptive parents as he was growing up. On the one hand, he was very special because of being "chosen," yet there was something about his adoption that could clearly not be talked about.

His Aunt Laurie lived out on the West Coast and visited rarely. He had always had the feeling when she visited that she and his (adoptive) mother did not like each other. He remembers her coming one Christmas with her husband and three children, all girls. He was about twelve at the time. They stayed at his maternal grandparents. He recalls very vividly that there was an air of strain over the whole household all the time that they were there. He could feel the relief in the air, he said, when his aunt and her family left for home. He clearly remembers that he had always felt his Aunt Laurie did not like him, though he cannot remember her ever being especially unkind. It was just "the way she spoke, and the way she would avoid looking at me."

She was the only member of his family who didn't come to his wedding three years ago. This seemed to confirm his life-long impression of her indifference.

When his wife became pregnant, he had told his adoptive mother

that he was seriously thinking of registering with the adoption agency
to try to find his birth mother. She became quite agitated and tried
hard to dissuade him, stressing the possibility of "shock and disappointment" if the circumstances were hard to understand, or if "the
woman" should reject his attempts at contact. She asked if she hadn't
done a "good enough job" of being his mother and took his concern
to find his birth mother as a rejection of her. He had done his best to
reassure her that this was not in any way a reflection on her. She was
his "real" mother, but knowing nothing about his own beginnings
had become over the years a sort of "black hole" in his heart and mind
which he longed to fill. The prospect of becoming a parent himself had
seemed to bring it to a head. His adoptive mother seemed somewhat
appeased by this, but had asked him to wait a while, because her
mother—Grandma Linaama—was very ill with cancer at the time, and
she thought it might upset her. He had agreed to wait a while, but
made it clear that his mind was made up to pursue his plans eventually, and told her that his wife supported him in this plan.

His son was born on December 4th, last year.

Just before Christmas, Aunt Laurie came to see her mother in
the hospital and his adoptive mother called and said that Grandma
would like to see him "specially." At the hospital, his grandmother
had told him that his Aunt Laurie had something special to talk to
him about, and that she was at his mother's. He should go there as
soon as he left the hospital. She told him how proud she had always
been of him, that he had been "one wonderful grandson" to her. They
had a very loving exchange in which he had told her he thought he
was a lucky person to have been made part of their family. She had
died about six weeks later.

The same evening he "dropped in on" his adoptive mother and
found her with his Aunt Laurie. At first they were both very tense but
gradually, becoming more relaxed, they told him that "Aunt Laurie"
had conceived him when she was seventeen. She was still in high
school. She had been quite determined to keep him and wanted to
quit school and get a job. Her parents felt that she had brought disgrace
on the family and insisted that she must give the baby up for adoption.
Her older sister (his adoptive mother) had learned just a year before
that it would be impossible for her to sustain a pregnancy because of
internal injuries resulting from a riding accident when she was in her
teens. She had had two miscarriages.

She and her husband offered to adopt Laurie's baby on the
strict conditions that she would never interfere, and would solemnly
promise never to tell him she was his birth mother. Laurie told him
that she agreed because it was a way "of not giving him up to strang-

ers," and because deep down she was frightened of the responsibility of trying to bring him up alone with no education or job training and no support from her family. She explained to him that, twenty-eight years ago, single parenthood wasn't accepted like it is today. The adoption had been legally completed through our agency.

Mark said that the whole encounter had been very intense and highly charged with emotion for them all. "We all cried together," he said. Grandma Linaama had told both women that it was time they told him the truth as a way of making up the estrangement they had allowed to grow between themselves. His adoptive mother had told Laurie how jealous she had been of her after her marriage, having three children of her own, and Laurie told her sister how much she had envied her for having "my only boy," and how hard it was to forgive her and her husband for the stern conditions they had set. Mark had tried to comfort both women by reassuring them that he didn't hold anything against either of them, but he did tell Laurie that he had always felt she didn't like him. Laurie wept bitterly and said when he was little she had just longed to grab him and run away with him, and as he got older she felt that she just had to "harden her heart" against the feeling that he was "really" hers. At times it hurt her just to look at him.

When he had finally asked what he felt was "the logical question" about who his father was and whether he had been in the picture when these decisions were made about his future, Laurie had become very tense and said she couldn't talk about that. His adoptive mother said it was best to leave that a "closed chapter" and had "almost begged" him to be satisfied with knowing the truth about his adoption. Since he had been given a lot of new things to digest, Mark said he did not pursue this further at the time.

However, the question about his father "will not go away," he said. He has been very much involved with his little boy's care from the day they brought him home. He showed me the baby's most recent picture with enjoyment and pride and says he wants very much to be a good father—the kind his own adoptive father had been when he was little.

He began to cry as he told me he remembers how terribly sad he was when his father died, and how frightened he had been when he realized he was angry at his dad for "going off and leaving me alone." He was afraid to talk to his adoptive mother about this, because he had a feeling that it was "a wicked thought." He remembers his maternal grandfather as being always kindly and humorous, but they never did things together because of grandfather's poor health. When he died, it brought back for a time all the distress of his father's death and he "went through a pretty bad time." By this he meant that he had nightmares about being alone in storms or lost in old buildings, and for a while he lost interest in school. One of his uncles had been very kind to him at that time and that had helped, but about a year later this uncle had been transferred by his company out to the West Coast, "So I lost him, too."

He has tried to think of the pros and cons of trying to locate his birth father, and wanted to talk all this over with me. His wife wishes that he would just let go of these longings, but he can't seem to do that.

He wondered if young men who had fathered a child in similar circumstances ever wondered about the child later on. What would be his father's reaction if Mark found out where he was and phoned and said, "I'm that son you had, remember?" I mentioned that Mark had sounded really angry as he said that. He swore and said that, looking at his own son, he just didn't see how a father could "just walk away." I said there were a lot of things to think and talk about. There was the possibility that Laurie had never named the father.[1] There was also the possibility that, if contacted, his father might refuse to meet Mark, not wanting to reopen something he had put completely behind him, or to deal with it in terms of his present life. Mark said, "It's possible, isn't it, that his name is on a file right here in this building somewhere?" and I said yes, it was possible. He said that gave him a very queer feeling, and I said I thought I could understand that. I said I would like to help Mark think these things through, and he agreed. We made an appointment for next week. He will talk to his wife about her coming, too.

---

1. Not necessarily a legal requirement in some jurisdictions.

PART FOUR

ADULT SERVICES

CHAPTER 16

Adult Child of an Alcoholic: Pauline Roszinski

Agency:
College Student Counseling Services.

Referral date:
February 12, 19xx.

Referral source:
Professor Madeleine Ruddick, School of Nursing, had suggested to Pauline that we could help her, and Pauline had agreed to make an appointment.

Family data:

Client:	Pauline Theresa Roszinski, age 25, born May 24, 19xx, the only child in her family.
Mother:	Elzbieta Roszinski, age 65, said to be in very poor health. Resident at Pinewood Manor, Keenesville.
Father:	Deceased, about three years ago in a car accident, then age 66.
Maternal Uncle:	John Krenz, age 66, listed by client as "next of kin" on college forms.

Background Information

Professor Ruddick said that Pauline has been quite depressed since getting her first semester grades back. She is in the second year of a baccalaureate program in nursing. In her first year, she failed the clinical course component and is repeating it this year. Her performance in clinical work last semester was erratic, occasionally up to standard but often below what it needs to be, and it has deteriorated since Christmas. Fall semester academic grades were also poor. The nursing faculty have told Pauline, with mid-semester evaluations approaching, that they are considering whether or not she should be allowed to continue in the program. Pauline had statedly agreed that Professor Ruddick should explain this to me. We agreed to meet on February 16, 19xx.

Intake Interview: February 16, 19xx

Pauline presented as a very shy, quiet young woman. She is about 5'4", slightly built, with medium brown hair, cut quite short, fine features and rather a "fragile" look about her. She has a habit of looking up at you with her head a little down and her chin pulled in— it is almost childlike. She was neatly but very plainly dressed, in a style that seemed to me a little "old-fashioned" by college student standards.

I told her I understood she knew that Professor Ruddick had told me the main points of her present situation, and I asked her to tell me what was most important about it for her. She said that Professor Ruddick suggested she ask our office for help with her depression about the exams and also with what is causing her difficulty in the nursing program. Professor Ruddick has told Pauline that she will recommend to her colleagues that Pauline continue in the program *provided she is getting counseling with us.* Pauline says the professor told her, "Don't worry! I'll fight for you!", adding that she expected Pauline "not to let her down."

I asked if she felt a bit "pushed" to come here but Pauline said quickly that she didn't at all. She thought it was very kind of Professor Ruddick to "bother with her," and that she really knew she had to have help because nothing seemed to be working out. I said I could understand that must be pretty frightening, and I asked her to tell me how it was affecting her.

Pauline said it isn't "frightening," it's just a bit worrying. She cannot sleep. She falls asleep all right but wakes up about four o'clock most mornings and cannot get back to sleep again. She just lies in bed and worries about things. When asked what things, she responded: flunking her exams, what she'll do if she has to get out of nursing, and how badly she feels for wasting her uncle's money (he is paying her way through college). He had even said that he had always wanted a daughter, but he had had three boys, and that was why he was covering the expense of her nursing degree. Besides, he had said, it was an investment; she would be able to look after him when he got old and sick. I noticed that while Pauline laughed as she said that, her eyes filled with tears, and her laugh ended in a sort of sob. I said that seemed to hurt her, and she stated that she obviously wasn't very good at looking after people and she hated to think she had "let him down." He is her "only real parent," she said.

In answer to my question, Pauline said her father and mother had separated when she was about fifteen. She had continued to live with her mother, but saw her father fairly regularly. They had not divorced, because they were devout Catholics "of the old school." They both were "people with problems of their own," and she had always felt that neither of them really was "there for her." Rather, it had always seemed that they needed her, even when she was little. But, of course, "They couldn't help it." In answer to my question about their "problems," Pauline hesitated, and said it was very hard to explain. I waited, and she went on to say that they both drank "quite a lot."

Her mother, who was forty when Pauline was born, had had almost constant pain from a "badly damaged uterus" after Pauline's birth. She had always told Pauline that "aspirins and things wouldn't touch it," and that she used alcohol to relieve the pain. When her mother became drowsy and helpless with the alcohol, Pauline looked after her—right from the time she was a little girl, because she believed that the pain was her fault "for being born." She guessed her father was "what you would call an alcoholic." He worked a steady 3:00 to 11:00 p.m. shift as a security guard at the steel plant in Keenesville where they lived. He only drank on weekends, but then it was steady from the morning on, for two days. She would clean up after him when he vomited and help him to bed. She used to stay awake and wait up for them when they had been out with friends or to a bar on Saturday nights. Sometimes they would go to bed then, but sometimes they would sit down and have some more drinks at home. When that happened she would lie awake, trying not to go to sleep, in case they fell asleep while smoking. She was always very afraid of fire. Once, when she was about seven or eight, she had woken up to the smell of smoke and had found her dad asleep in his chair. The inside of the chair, between the arm and the seat cushion was smoldering from a cigarette he had dropped.

I said it sounded like she had had a pretty tough time growing up. She said it wasn't really so bad, but it was a bit "lonely." She did fairly well in school, she "got through all right," but it was "lonely" because she could never mix comfortably with the other kids, and she used to worry about her mom at home alone. She never took part in afterschool sports or activities because she had to get home to take care of her mom.

When she was eighteen, she decided to quit school, rather than take the last year that would give her college entrance, as she didn't think her marks were good enough, and she saw no prospect of being able to afford college. She decided to enter a convent and become a nun. She said she realized now that this was very wrong of her, because she did it "just to get away from home." She knew she did not really have a vocation, but hoped that this would come if she applied herself to the convent discipline. Her mother had bitterly opposed her going at first, crying that now she would have nobody to care for her. But Pauline said she felt very harsh towards her mother at that time, and felt she had done her bit for so many years and wanted her own life. She now felt that this was selfish and "very wrong of me." Once her plans were firm, her mother began to boast to her friends about her daughter entering the religious life, although privately to Pauline she still complained about "being left all alone and in constant pain."

She remained in the convent for almost two years. She remembers that it was "very peaceful and such an orderly life," and in many ways she was happy there. From time to time, her mother would get ill and send for her, and Mother Superior would give her "leave" to go home and look after her. Sometimes she would find that her mother wasn't really as sick as she had led her to believe, but Pauline said she didn't dare to take a chance of refusing to go home, for fear it was really something serious.

She had some difficulties with the discipline. Not that she was rebellious, she told me, only it didn't seem to have any real meaning for her. The Mistress of Novices began to talk to her about her lack of "earnestness and conviction" and very kindly suggested that she was not really ready for the religious life at this time. This woman had seemed to be very warm and gentle at first, and Pauline began to trust that she would help her become more suited to the life of a nun. But instead she realized that the Mistress and another senior nun were intent on confronting her with their belief that she wasn't ready to be a nun and that she had better leave. They were kind about it, she said, and so was Mother Superior, but they were "very firm."

She had no choice but to leave, and although she dreaded returning because she was so ashamed of her "failure," she went back to her mother's home.

Her mother made dreadful scenes about Pauline's "failure" at the convent; how she had "let her down" in the sight of her friends,

"What can I tell them?" and so forth. Pauline still feels very guilty about the whole experience, and she feels very ashamed of how angry she was, inside, that her mother couldn't understand what the "failure" meant to her. She had gone through a bad time, not sleeping well, and having crying jags that she couldn't explain, and just feeling very "down" about everything for about six months. She went to church a lot, and felt it did help, although she felt ashamed all the time about not being "truly religious" like the other worshippers.

She got various jobs clerking in stores, and took a business computer course at night so that she could get some secretarial work. She had tried to help her parents budget their combined incomes, so that they could live more comfortably, but her mother resented this and became very secretive about the money, so she stopped trying. She had liked the secretarial job that she obtained and she "guessed" she had done fairly well. She got promoted to a more responsible position—but added quickly that it was "just because another young woman got pregnant and they needed someone to fill her slot." Pauline said the firm was "very generous" in the reference they gave her when she left. I asked if they were more generous than she deserved and she said firmly, "Oh yes, I wasn't that good. I made lots of mistakes." She lived at home for almost three years.

When her uncle retired he made plans to move back to Keenesville, where he and her mother had grown up, and renewed contact with Pauline and her parents. His visits meant a lot to her, and when he and her aunt moved back, she felt welcome in their home and it became a bright spot in her life.

Her father was killed in a car accident not long after this, almost three years ago. It seemed he was very drunk and drove the car into a highway bridge abutment. Her mother's condition deteriorated from that point, and she became almost mentally ill. She had a couple of very bad falls which rendered her partially disabled. She was quite unable to remain alone at home during the day while Pauline went out to work. Pauline's uncle apparently took over at that point and placed his sister in a specialized long-term care home. He sold his sister's home, investing Pauline's share, and she went to live with her uncle and aunt.

It was then, almost two years ago now, that he told Pauline he would give her a college education if she wanted it. He paid for her to take some aptitude and interest tests at a college in Keenesville. Pauline said that her strongest "lines" were in business and communications, but nursing, with emphasis on care of the elderly, also featured in her profile.

She had thought nursing would be wonderful—she would enjoy

looking after sick people and making them feel better. She had liked sciences at school, and math had been her best subject, so she didn't think those aspects of the program would pose any problem. But it hadn't worked out, and here she was. "It's all my fault—I've bombed out again."

I said I could understand her feeling that way, but it seemed to me that all it really meant was that she just hadn't found the right path for herself yet. I would like to help her look at what had gone wrong and why things hadn't worked out. I said I believed that much of what had happened was by no means "all her fault." I pointed out that most young people who had grown up with alcoholic parents carried a lot of pain inside, and had difficulty finding a path to become their real self, and particularly in learning how to be good to themselves. I asked if she had heard of the group that Student Counseling Services had started this year for adult children of alcoholics. Pauline said she had heard someone mention it, but she had heard it was just for people who had had to go into child-protective care because of their parents' drinking, and besides, she said, "It was only my father who was alcoholic." Her mother just "took wine and brandy for the pain."

I said that it sounded to me like her mother was addicted to alcohol, and that alcohol had seemed to cause problems in her mother's life, which was AA's definition of an alcoholic. Pauline looked down at her hands and said, almost in wonder, "Perhaps." I said we could talk more about that, and the other things she was struggling with next time.

I explained that I would like to see her again one week from today, she agreed and we set a mutually convenient time.

CHAPTER 17

Aging: Clifford and Jean Roberts

Agency:
>   Family Service Center, Lakesford (pop. 150,000).

Referral source:
>   Self, Mrs. Jean Roberts, by phone.

Referral date:
>   October 4, 19xx.

Family data:
>   *Client:* Jean Roberts, age 46.
>   *Husband:* Clifford Roberts, age 50.
>   *Children:* Mark, age 26, computer programmer, in a distant city.
>   Ian, age 23, in graduate school at a university in a distant city.
>   Paula, age 21, in senior year, B.S. (physics), at Lakesford University.

Mrs. Roberts called and made an appointment to talk about the care of her husband's mother, now aged seventy-five, who has lived with them for six years. I wondered if she and her husband would like to come together, but she was quite insistent that she come alone the first time. We set an appointment for October 18, 19xx.

Intake Interview: October 18, 19xx

Mr. Roberts' father died of cancer nine years ago and his mother remained in her own home in a community ninety-four miles away for almost two and a half years until her health began to be a problem, at which point she moved in with Clifford and Jean.

Clifford is the youngest of two siblings. His older sister is widowed, and is a high school principal on the east coast. Having married somewhat later in life, she still has two children living at home. At the time of his father's death, Clifford promised him that he would "always look after mother."

I learned then that Mrs. Roberts had not told her husband that she was coming to the agency for advice.

She feels his mother's care has become a tremendous burden, and resents what she feels is "carrying all the load of Cliff's promise to his dad—it doesn't cost *him* anything." The senior Mrs. Roberts' health has been deteriorating over the past two years. She has frequent bouts of very severe bronchitis, chronic constipation, and migraine headaches. A heavy smoker, she refuses any and all suggestions from her doctor, let alone the family, that this is affecting her health. She has become very forgetful and, in fact, this was one of the main reasons they felt she could no longer live alone in her own house. Often she asks the same question over and over again, although they may have answered it a few minutes before. Sometimes it almost seems as if she is "not with it" for perhaps an hour at a time, then she will come round and appear quite normal for perhaps two or three days. Occasionally she will turn on them with very cruel, cutting remarks about their life-style, upbringing of the children, and so forth.

One of the most demanding aspects of her mother-in-law's care, for Jean, is that Mrs. Roberts senior will not stay alone in the house at all. Furthermore, she insists that one of the family stay with her, not a homemaker or a sitter. Last winter this became a tremendous burden on the family.

According to Jean, last winter, Mrs. Roberts senior insisted on coming along on every errand or outing during the day. This meant helping her with her winter coat, boots, etc. and helping her into the car. She is not very mobile, partly because she refuses to obey the doctor's instructions to walk in the summer and to do leg exercises in the house in the winter.

When Jean and Cliff want to go out in the evening, they have to get Paula to come and stay. Otherwise one of them must stay at home with her. Last winter, Paula lived at home and this made it a little easier for them, but she moved into an apartment with a friend in July, and naturally is not as readily available for sitting in with her grandmother. Jean dreads the winter coming on, and is beginning to feel more and more trapped in the situation.

"Just when I could have given some thought to myself, I'm stuck with all this," she told me. When she tries to broach the matter with her husband, he becomes very upset, reminds her of his promise to his father, and makes her feel very guilty about her feelings of resentment.

The situation is now affecting their relationship. Shared activities they once enjoyed are now impossible. Going to church creates much the same problem as going out in the evening. They must go separately on alternate Sundays as Mrs. Roberts senior has refused to go to their church ever since the minister preached a sermon of which she disapproved.

Jean wants information about nursing homes in the area. She also wants me to tell her husband that it is too much for her, and that he should begin taking his mother out to look at local facilities for the aged.

CHAPTER 18

Incest: Marla Gerritsen[1]

Agency:
University Counseling Services in a small college (student pop. 3,000) in a medium-sized industrial city (pop. 130,000).

Referral date:
February 16, 19xx.

Referral source:
Self, Marla Gerritsen.

Intake interview:
February 24, 19xx.

Presenting Problem

Marla, aged twenty-three years, is a graduate student in psychology. She has fine features, large brown eyes, and short, straight dark brown hair. Her appearance at the interview was quite unkempt. Her hair looked uncared for, her blouse was obviously not clean, and it was missing a button in the front. She hunched her shoulders, "slouched" into the room, and sat in a hunched over position in the chair.

She told me that lately, she has found it increasingly difficult to concentrate on her studies. The workload is admittedly heavy, but until this term she has had no more than the normal amount of difficulty with her courses.

She is not sleeping well, and most mornings awakens at about

---

1. This case was written by Patricia P. Millar, L.C.S.W., Case Manager, Domiciliary Homeless Program, V.A. Medical Center, Little Rock, AR.

four thirty or five o'clock a.m. and just lies there worrying about how to get her work done. However, on the one or two occasions on which she has gotten up, made some coffee and tried to work, she has found that what she reads "does not make any sense," and although she reads it over and over again, she has not understood it, nor was she able to take useful notes. This has made her very angry, she told me. In response to my question, she said she is not sure who she is angry at or what she is angry about. "At myself for being so dumb, perhaps; at these 'brilliant writers' who want you to think they're so clever and don't believe anybody is ever going to understand their work!" Marla spat out with sarcastic bitterness.

Background Information

Marla has very few friends. "I'm a loner," she said, adding that she just hasn't the time for socializing because her workload is too heavy this year. However, she admits that she did not do much socializing in her undergraduate years, either. Her eyes filled with tears at this point, and she choked up as she told me that she really didn't like getting "too close" to other people. She has never felt she "fit in with the crowd." She feels "different" from other girls her own age, and finds the young male students "very immature."

In response to my asking her to explain "different," Marla cried bitterly and told me a story of repeated sexual experiences she had had with her paternal uncle from age thirteen until she left home for college at age eighteen.

Uncle Mike owned a movie theater in her hometown and when she was thirteen she had gone to work for him in the popcorn/soft drinks/candy concession at the theater. She worked on weekends and during school summer breaks. At the time she went to work for him her uncle was thirty-two years old and had been married for six months. A handsome, flamboyant man, he had been her hero for as long as she could remember.

He always drove her home after the show so that her parents would not worry about her being out unescorted at night. What started out as light petting soon led to intercourse. Uncle Mike would ask her to come up into the projection room while the movie was running, although this necessitated her leaving the concession stand to the other two girls who worked there. These girls, Kate and Anne, resented the special attention Mike paid her and of the time he allowed her away from the counter, but Marla said she rather enjoyed flaunting her special status and making her friends jealous. She told them she was previewing movies with her uncle in the projection room.

Marla has never told her parents, nor anyone else about her uncle's relations with her. At first it was "fun" to be thirteen years old and to think about her and Uncle Mike's "special secret." When she was about fifteen, a boy in her class at school wanted to date her, but her uncle discouraged this, and told her he was just "a kid from the boonies." She didn't need his attention, she was "too much woman for a schoolboy," and anyway she had a "real man" in him. Marla remembers that she felt flattered by this, as if she was "above" the high school dating crowd. Sometimes, however, later on in high school, she felt left out, never having a date for parties and so on, and began to resent Uncle Mike's feeling that he "owned" her exclusively. But then he would give her a generous gift of money, and she would give in and continue the relationship with him.

Leaving home for college was a "relief" from this pressure and there have been no more incidents since then. She is careful, as far as she possibly can, never to be alone with her uncle. She said that leaving home sort of convinced her that she didn't have to keep on with the relationship and, in fact, she has become increasingly resentful of her uncle and barely speaks to him on the rare occasions she sees him.

She has never told anyone about it, and has tried to "put the whole thing behind me." However, from time to time, her studies in psychology have made her wonder if she can be mentally healthy by just "repressing" it all.

Last November she and a couple of her classmates watched a program on TV about a woman whose father had been incestuous with her for years. She found it almost impossible to remain watching as this now grown woman's distress was shown in the program very graphically. Her friends' reaction disturbed her intensely also. They were filled with compassion for the woman's hatred of her father's sexual actions and her sense of powerlessness, as a child, in the face of this terrifying experience. They discussed afterwards whether a woman could ever have a "normal" attitude about sex after such treatment.

This experience had been very upsetting to her. It had "stirred it all up again," and she began to feel terribly ashamed about having actually enjoyed the sexual relations with her uncle. She feels that if anyone ever knew this, her peers, both men and women, would completely reject her.

At home this past Christmas, her uncle, who had had quite a lot to drink, made a pass at her in the kitchen. She had told him to leave her alone, and when he persisted, she threatened to tell his wife, her parents and everyone. Her uncle sneered at her and said, "Who's going to believe you? You teased and flirted with me until I gave it to you and you loved it, didn't you? Don't try to be Miss Prim-and-Proper with me!"

Marla said that this has convinced her that she can never expose her uncle. For one thing, too many people might be hurt by it—his wife, their two children, her parents. As well, she would be publicly shamed by being labelled as having complied willingly.

CHAPTER 19

Adult Probation: Randy Kimball

Agency:
Probation Service, Special Needs Division, in a medium-sized industrial city (pop. 130,000).

Referral date:
November 29, 19xx.

Referral source:
Criminal Court, Judge Norman LeFebvre, via Probation Service Intake Department.

Family data:
Client: Randy Kimball, age 24, born Dec. 10, 19xx.
Wife: Cheryl (Garry) Kimball, age 25, born Jan. 15, 19xx.

Presenting Problem:

Randy was placed on probation on November 29, 19xx, having been before the court on his third charge of assault. Although this assault was more serious than the two former ones, the judge decided on a probation order rather than a jail sentence because of Randy's developmental handicap, and because his older brother was present and told the court that Randy could come home and live with him and his wife. The terms of the probation order are:

1. Stay out of bars and only drink at his brother's home;
2. Attend at the probation office for counseling;
3. Take his medication regularly;
4. Attend anger management classes at the Mental Health Clinic.

Background Information

Randy is developmentally handicapped and cannot read or write. However, he can function normally in most areas. He is able to, and has, lived independently. He is on a tranquilizer to control his mood swings and to curb his aggressiveness, but he often "forgets" to take this medication. He is said to drink heavily at times, and admits that it was because of his drinking that his wife, Cheryl, left him about two months ago. They have been married since last February. He has lived alone since she left.

Randy was employed at the local Sheltered Workshop for almost two years, but they had to let him go because of his aggressiveness. This was in November of last year.

As a child, Randy had petit mal seizures but he grew out of this at puberty. The medical record (part of the presentence report) also states that he was referred to a psychiatrist by the court at the time of his first charge, in June, two years ago, but the psychiatrist said there was really nothing he could do for a developmentally handicapped person.

Randy believes that if Cheryl had stayed with him he would not have gotten into a fight with the other man. It is really Cheryl's fault that he is in trouble with the law again. I noticed that he smiled broadly as he described that the other guy's nose was broken and "I bloodied him up pretty good, I guess." He says he got mad because the other man teased him about Cheryl having left, and taunted him about being sexually unequal to the needs of a "hot one" like Cheryl.

Randy lived with his parents until he went into a group home at age twenty-two. That was when he began working at the Sheltered Workshop. He stayed in the group home until he was twenty-four, when he and another young man found an apartment and went out on their own. This was about a year ago. The arrangement lasted for about two months, but they were asked to leave by the landlord because of frequent fights and noise. He then found an efficiency for himself and lived alone there until he met Cheryl. They met and married in "a few weeks." Cheryl works in a small restaurant. Randy thinks she went as far as ninth grade, and says she is "a lot smarter than I am at reading and stuff." He does not take his medication regularly because "sometimes it muddles my head."

Observations

Randy is about six feet tall with dark hair and blue eyes. He is well-built and gives an impression of muscular strength. He wears rather thick glasses. He appears well-groomed and clean and neat in his dress. I noticed that he wore attractive cowboy boots on this occasion.

His manner is pleasant and outwardly cooperative, but he often attributes difficulties to other persons or events. For example, it was Cheryl's fault he has faced this charge; he had to leave the Sheltered Workshop because the supervisor was a "rotten S.O.B.," and didn't know as much about the work as Randy did, and that made the supervisor "hate me because I showed him up all the time." Also, his former landlord was "one of these religious types" who thought a bit of beer was the "devil's wickedness" and couldn't stand him and his friend "having a few" on a weekend.

Randy says his brother is very good to him, but his sister-in-law is a "bit old-fashioned in her ways." By this he meant that she didn't like him swearing, and that she had convinced his brother that two beers on weekend evenings was the limit. Randy thinks this is "fanatic."

CHAPTER 20

Rape: Celene Horvath[1]

Agency:
Community Mental Health Services in Lakesford, a medium-sized industrial city (pop. 150,000).

Referral date:
June 14, 19xx.

Referral source:
Self, Ms. Horvath, on the suggestion of her friend, Jenny Mallory, a former client of this agency.

Note: Ms. K. Zavitz, a staff member of this agency, had taken part in a local TV program concerning date rape, following which Ms. Mallory had contacted her out of concern for her friend, Celene Horvath. Ms. Zavitz had suggested she have Ms. Horvath call the agency for an appointment.

Intake Interview

I met Celene Horvath on June 26, 19xx. She is thirty-seven years of age, single, and works as a sales supervisor for a business machine company here in Lakesford. She presented as a well-dressed, personable, professional woman, with a pleasant manner in the interview situation. Outwardly, she seems quite relaxed. However, I noted that she continually twisted one foot around on the floor, and she clasped her hands tightly on her lap, and never moved them until about half an hour into the interview.

1. This case was written by Patricia P. Millar, L.C.S.W., Case Manager, Domiciliary Homeless Program, V.A. Medical Center, Little Rock, AR.

Presenting Problem

Celene is struggling with the personal aftermath of a date rape experience. She is "constantly tired" and this is beginning to affect her work. She goes to bed early—sometimes as early as 6:30 p.m.—only to awaken at 8:30 or 9 p.m., and then is unable to get back to sleep until 2:00 or 3:00 a.m. She frequently has horrifying nightmares. She has completely given up any social life, because to park her car in her apartment's underground parking lot at night is simply too terrifying. She has lost her appetite and rarely cooks a proper meal for herself more than once or twice a week.

Until recently she has been very proud of her success with the company, which was achieved, she said, by her own hard work and effort. Her feelings are affecting her work in that she has lost confidence in her ability to make decisions, and this extends into her personal life as well.

Six weeks ago, Celene attended a one-week national sales meeting in New York. On the last night of the meetings, another sales supervisor whom she had met occasionally at meetings in the past invited her to go to dinner with him. Although they had never dated before, she had talked to him at previous meetings and found him an interesting person.

Before they were to go to dinner, Ed invited Celene to his room for a drink. She said they had a lively, enjoyable conversation and consumed several drinks in a short period of time. She said they were "flirting a lot" and a couple of times she expressed concern to Ed about "where it might lead." He had just laughed at her, poured more drinks for them both, and the "party" continued.

At some point, Celene recalled, Ed was sitting beside her on the bed. Quite suddenly, he pulled her backwards and, partially lying on top of her, began to kiss her "hard and passionately."

She said she tried to resist and to get up, but she was really quite dizzy and weak. He then began undressing her and she feebly tried to fight him off. He became very angry and called her a "prick tease" and said he would "teach her a lesson."

Ed then viciously raped her. She was by then very fearful and did not resist him. When he had finished, he said to her, "See? I knew you really wanted it. I could tell the first moment I met you what you were like." Celene said she got up and stumbled to the bathroom where she vomited violently. She put on her dress, and carrying her underclothes, returned to her own room, shocked, hurt, frightened, and disgusted. Nothing like this had ever happened to her before. She collapsed on her bed, in her dress, and slept until 1:30 a.m., when she awoke and took a long shower. However, she could not go back to sleep and lay awake until morning.

Although a company breakfast had been scheduled to close the meeting, Celene did not attend and arranged for an earlier flight back to Lakesford. As she was leaving the hotel, she saw Ed in the lobby talking with several men. He gave her a "knowing wink" and continued his conversation with the other men. She said she was frightened at the sight of him, wishing that he would have forgotten the incident, just as she intended to do. Unfortunately, she has found herself unable to do this.

Ever since this experience, Celene has stopped any social contact with men, and says she is actually physically uncomfortable in male company. She often looks in the mirror, trying to see just what Ed saw the first time he looked at her, and she tries to think about how she had tantalized him. She is even avoiding social contacts with women, because she feels so afraid of "what they might think if they knew about her." Whenever she awakens from sleep, she has a sudden feeling of dread in the pit of her stomach. It is this feeling, she says, that is preventing her from wanting to eat, and she has lost about nine pounds in the six weeks since this experience.

Celene told me she has no intention of reporting the rape, since she feels she "played such a large part in it." She is concerned about possible effects on her career if she reports it, and feels it wouldn't be fair to Ed either, since it might affect his seventeen-year career with the company.

PART FIVE

COMMUNITY AND GROUP WORK

CHAPTER 21

Community Problem: Beaver Creek Reservation

Agency:

Social Planning, Research, and Advisory Council, in a region comprising a rural population and a medium-sized industrial city (pop. 125,000).

Referral date:

June 8, 19xx.

Referral source:

Beaver Creek Band Council. Population on the reservation is 1,500.

Presenting Problem

Chief Morningstar and the Band Council are very concerned about problems on the reservation. He and elders Joseph Swiftfoot and Margaret Pangwatin came to the agency by appointment to discuss if there were ways in which we could help them. They were accompanied by Roy Onsawin, a young artist who grew up on the reservation, went away to college, and has recently returned to live in Birchville. He is interested in helping with the difficulties they are experiencing. He and his wife, herself a talented native craftswoman, operate a picture-framing business in Birchville, where they also sell his paintings and her pottery and beadwork.

The Band Council feel there is widespread depression and a feeling of hopelessness among the residents of the reservation. The older people feel the youth have no respect for their elders and no knowledge of, or respect for, their native heritage. Attempts to bring about change have been made. For example, Ms. Pangwatin had

101

started an evening group for children ages ten to thirteen to study the Band's history, folklore, legends, and language; but since the recent disturbances parents have refused to let the children attend.

Unemployment is high—78 percent—on the reservation and many families are on general welfare assistance. There is a lot of heavy drinking and some family violence.

Social services such as Alcoholics Anonymous (AA), welfare administration, and child welfare services, who come on to the reservation from Birchville, are resented and regarded with suspicion, although recently two prominent Band members who carry some influence have joined AA and this has helped. While there is resentment of the child welfare authority, most band members realize that neglect and ill-treatment of children has to be dealt with under the law. However, the removal of children from their parents' care, and their subsequent placement in the city, usually in non-native foster homes, is bitterly resented. The general feeling is, "They (the outside white agency workers) look down on us and don't understand our ways." The exception is the Public Health nurse, who, though not from Beaver Creek, is herself native, and is fairly well accepted.

The Chief said that there had been a lot of problems on the reservation over the winter, and things had come to a head over a period of time since January. On New Year's Day, the body of Theresa M., seventeen years of age, was found in a ditch beside an isolated stretch of road near Green Creek Falls. The pathologist's report stated that Theresa had been drinking heavily and had also taken drugs during the last hours of her life; enough probably to produce unconsciousness, but not, in his opinion, to cause death. It appeared that she had had a very severe fall, perhaps from the road and then through the ice into the ditch. She had hit her head and right shoulder on rocks that edged the ditch but had probably died as a result of exposure over several hours in the icy water of the ditch that was approximately two feet deep. The temperature that night in the area was about fifteen degrees Fahrenheit. There was no evidence of sexual assault. The coroner's jury had ruled the cause of death as unknown. There had been rumors and hinted accusations among residents on the reservation, but police investigations had been inconclusive. They (the police) had told the Chief it was their impression that "no one would talk."

Other problems include teenage suicide. Since the New Year, there had been three suicides of teenagers on the reservation. One had left a note saying, in part, "There's nothing to live for, no one will miss me."

Residents are concerned and even afraid, because the young people, most in their late teens, out of school and unemployed, go off the reservation to drink—usually at the Moonbeam Tavern on Highway 143. They then tear about the reservation on motorcycles and in cars, "looking for trouble," and getting into fights. (There seem to be two rival "gangs.") It is rumored that some are on drugs, but again, police investigations have led nowhere.

When I asked what kind of "trouble," the Chief said it was mainly vandalism—tearing down fences, letting the air out of people's tires, stealing hubcaps, that sort of thing. However, once they had apparently set fire to quite a large pile of brush behind a house, which, if the owner had not come home in time, and if it had been a windy night, would have set the house on fire. On another occasion, they had apparently encircled the home of a rival gang member at about midnight, and had created a great din of shouting and banging on the sides of the house until the residents had come on the porch to protest. Then, waiting until the lights went out, the young people had returned and started up the noise again. This had been repeated three times. A neighbor with a phone had called the police, but by the time they arrived, all was quiet and no cars or young people were to be seen. Another time they had removed the back steps of the house of an elderly couple and the woman of the house had a bad fall the next morning when she went out to feed her chickens. She had been in the hospital for several weeks. She was the grandmother of a known gang member.

The Chief said that while nothing could be proved concerning who was responsible for these incidents, some neighbors had said they had seen young people, whom they could not, or would not, identify, tearing about on motorcycles in the vicinity of these residences on the relevant dates. Also, some gang members, always unnamed, are said to have boasted about the fire and how they "got back" at their rivals. Police had questioned several young people, and some of the older residents in the area, but as in their investigation of Theresa M.'s death, it was their impression that no one would talk.

The reservation is rife with rumors and accusations and residents are taking sides. The older people are afraid to go out at night. Some parents are not allowing their younger children to go to school because the children, having heard their parents talk, are getting into fights on the school bus and as they walk to and from school. Attendance at AA meetings has also fallen off and a group of women who had met to form a group for the study of native handicrafts has disbanded because of the bitterness between various factions. Most recently the dissension has even spread into the Council. The Chief and those with him today all said they feel that community life is breaking down.

The Council is split about the causes of the teenage unrest and about solutions to the problem. While some members urge the need for more links and acculturation with the outside white community, others want to maintain and even increase, if possible, their isolation. This latter group argues that a return to traditional values and practices is the only way for them to "have some say" in managing things on the reservation.

One hopeful sign has been that four of the younger men who have steady jobs and stable family lives have recently come to the Chief to share their concern about what is happening on the reservation and asked what they might do to change things. They believe that a Drop-In Center for young people might be a start and that providing some alternative activities for the teenagers would, in time, draw out those young people who don't really want to go along with the "wild element," but who presently see no alternative. The schoolhouse at Green Creek has been closed for five years. It is not in good shape and would need some repair, but could be made usable.

I told the Council members that our agency would certainly like to help them with some of the things they were struggling with, but I was concerned because we didn't have a native worker on our staff. I wondered if a white worker, however well qualified, might not add to the difficulties, rather than helping to solve them. They all agreed that while this might be an obstacle, they desperately need some expert help and did not know where to turn among their own people.

I did not at this time tell them, for fear of raising false hopes, that one of our staff members had taught school for three years on a native reservation in another state. I felt that I would need to discuss with this worker whether or not we could assign him to Beaver Creek. His experience could be helpful to them either directly, or in consultation, if his workload did not allow him to take on the assignment.

CHAPTER 22

Community Problem:
Hari Bindranath

Agency:
Social Work Services in the Housing Authority of Lakesford, a medium-sized industrial city (pop. 150,000).

Referral date:
April 4, 19xx.

Referral source:
Dale Gledden, M.S.W., school social worker with the Board of Education.

Family data:
Mother: Sharla Bindranath, age 34, born November 27, 19xx.
Father: Viswan Bindranath, deceased for 7 months.
Children: Hari (client), age 13 years, born October 17, 19xx.
Marilynne, age 9 years, born June 24, 19xx.
Stephanie, age 7 years, born March 4, 19xx.

Reason for Referral

Hari Bindranath was referred to Dr. George Carling, the school psychologist, by his homeroom teacher at Rosefield Elementary School. After seeing Hari, Dr. Carling referred him to the school social worker, because he felt it was a social environment situation that was causing this boy's difficulties. Mr. Gledden, the school social worker, believes the problems cannot be fully resolved without some intervention at a community level by our services. Mr. Gledden gave the following information:

Hari came to Rosefield School after the Christmas break, in good academic standing, in the seventh grade. His previous school (McConnell Memorial, in the steel mill area), reported him to be an industrious and cheerful student, performing slightly above average and getting along well with his classmates.

Since coming to Rosefield, his teachers have noticed a very marked deterioration in his grades and general work performance, and he appears "jumpy" and anxious in class. He hangs around the halls at recess and seems very reluctant to go out, and his anxiety seems to increase as the time for going home approaches.

His mother had told Dr. Carling that Hari is having nightmares and—more recently—stomach upsets. She had taken him to their family doctor but he had not found any physical cause for this.

Hari had not told his mother, but had with some difficulty told Dr. Carling, that he is being bullied by a group of boys somewhat older than him, some of whom are in the same grade at school. The bullying takes place both when they are at home in the housing complex and during recess at school. They call him "Paki" and "Brownie" and threaten to set fire to his little sister "like Pakis do." They stole his jacket and a baseball cap his dad had given him for his birthday the day before he died.

A couple of times recently, after dark, when he was babysitting his little sisters who had gone to bed, some of these boys began throwing things at the windows, jumping up and down on the little patio at the front, and rattling the door handles on the front and back doors. When Hari went to the door, they ran off yelling, "Yeah! Whacky Paki!" etc., only to begin again when he went back into the house.

Intake Interview

On April 13, 19xx, I met with Mrs. Bindranath. Mrs. Bindranath said that she and her two children moved into the Ellesmere Gardens public housing complex on the first of January this year. Her husband had died of a heart attack on the evening of October 18th last year.

Because they had been living in one of the older company houses near the steel mill, they were required to move when Mr. Bindranath no longer worked at the mill. The company had been very considerate and had given them enough time to get their name in to the Housing Authority and Mr. Bindranath's union had spoken to us, giving a good reference about the family's standards.

They are the first East Indians to move into Ellesmere Gardens. A neighbor has recently told Mrs. Bindranath that the former tenants of their unit were a single mother with two teenage children, who had been given notice to vacate because of destruction to the property and a lot of rowdiness that had disturbed the neighbors. The unit had been a "hang-out" for the younger teenagers in the complex, and the police had been called several times because of noise and fighting. The neighbors felt the kids were allowed to drink by Ms. Hoskins (the former tenant), but this had never been proven to the police.

As noted above, Hari had not told his mother about the bullying described above, but Mrs. Bindranath had become very concerned when Hari had told her on several occasions since coming to the housing complex that he wanted to quit school and get a job to help the family financially. She didn't know whom to go to for advice. She and her husband have always wanted the children to get a good education, and they saw that the opportunity was here for them.

The family emigrated from India ten years ago and came to Lakesford because there was work at the steel mill. They are the first of their family to leave India, but she hopes that her husband's brother and brother-in-law may be coming at some time in the future. She misses her family, but has made some friends among the local East Indian community who were very kind and helpful when Mr. Bindranath died.

She said that she herself has found some of her neighbors friendly, but there were some who "looked right through her" as though she wasn't there when she had tried to speak to them, waiting for the bus, and so on.

She and the children really like living in the complex in many ways. The new house is much nicer and more convenient than their old one near the steel mill, and she notices that some of the tenants have flowers around the houses. She is saving some money now for flower seeds. If it were not for Hari's unhappiness, she feels she could make a good life for the four of them, and carry out the dreams her husband had for his family in their new country.

CHAPTER 23

Group Work: Bereaved Parents Group

Agency:
Family Counseling Service: district office in a large town, with a population of 25,000.

Client group:
Four couples, each having lost a child under eight years of age from illness or accident in the past year. The group was initially set up because two of these couples came to the agency for counseling on the advice of their family doctors. Of the other two, one learned of the group's formation through their priest and the other came in response to the very strong suggestion of their sister-in-law, who is a public health nurse in Lakesford (the nearest city).

Purpose of the group:
Handling and resolving grief reaction through sharing of experiences and feelings.

Commencement date:
November 2, 19xx.

Group Participants

Jim and Pauline Rowland

Their youngest daughter Melissa, age four years, died four months ago of encephalitis. They have two older children, a boy age seven and a girl age ten.

Pat and Maureen Haggerty

Their only child Christopher, a boy age two and a half, drowned in the family pool last August. Mr. Haggerty was out of town on business at the time. His wife was with Christopher by the pool when the phone rang. She was expecting her husband to call long distance and had an urgent message for him to call his assistant manager here in town. Chris was playing some way off around the pool from where she was sitting, and she called to him to come with her and not to go near the pool, but in her haste she did not ensure that he had followed her. She thinks that he may have started to run after her and perhaps fell into the pool. By the time she had hung up the phone and run outside, he was face-down in the pool. She tried what resuscitation measures she and a neighbor knew, and then drove him to the hospital emergency room, but he was pronounced dead on arrival there. Both are devout Roman Catholics.

David and Moira Jackson

Their youngest child, Anne, a girl age eight, died in an asthmatic attack. She was born severely brain-damaged, had never been able to sit up, talk or feed herself, and had frequently suffered from severe respiratory problems with the slightest cold. They have three other children, all boys, ages eleven, fourteen and sixteen.

Maurice and Katherine Parker

Their third child and only son, Jason, died in his crib at age two and a half months. They have two daughters, ages three and six years. The death had occurred on New Year's Eve when they had an overnight baby-sitter. Because of the late hour of their return, they had "looked in on" but did not really check the baby when they came home.

Each of these couples had had an intake interview and one subsequent interview at which the group's formation and purpose was discussed.

First Meeting

At the first meeting, I recognized with them that the circumstances of their loss were, in each family, very different. In our area, to wait until other couples were located whose circumstances were similar could mean a long delay. While more homogeneous groups might become available a little sooner in Lakesford, one could not predict this with any certainty and the driving conditions during winter could mean they could not attend as regularly as if the group was here in Benton. I told them I believed that in spite of their different circumstances of loss, the open sharing of feelings and trying to understand each other could be a very real help to all of them. I would rely on them to let the group know if they felt that it was not helping them, and whether or not there was anything we could do to make it more effective. If it was felt this was not feasible, each of them would then, of course, be free to leave the group and could continue in individual counseling with the agency.

I suggested that we hold three meetings and then review together where we should go from there. I polled each member individually and, as all agreed to this plan, we wrote it up as a contract and they all signed their copy.

By the end of the second meeting the following has become clear:

1. The Parkers are blaming themselves a great deal although the autopsy showed typical sudden infant death syndrome (SIDS). In answer to Pauline Rowland's question, both had replied that they had "celebrated New Year's just like everyone else" but Mrs. Parker had perceived this as a not-very-subtle insinuation that they had had too much to drink and had added defensively that Maurice had driven them home "with no difficulty."

2. The Rowlands have a tendency to ask questions and to make observations that subtly imply "maybe you were to blame?" This is particularly noticeable in their comments to the Parkers, and to Maureen Haggerty. Pauline Rowland quite openly and deliberately shut Maureen out of one exchange, saying "You couldn't possibly understand how it felt to be completely helpless in the face of a critical illness due to medical incompetence," and she turned away to address the Jacksons. David Jackson looked pointedly at me at that moment. I felt very uncomfortable but said nothing. I noticed that Pat Haggerty took his wife's hand and held it.

3. Maureen Haggerty clearly blames herself for—as she puts it— "doing everything wrong," including not ensuring Christopher's safety in leaving him, losing her head when she found him at the bottom of the pool, and trying with her neighbor to resuscitate him for too long before calling an ambulance or getting him to the hospital. It is significant that Pat does not seem to blame her at all. He has suggested more than once that she needs to stop "whipping herself with what she might have done." He

told the group that he had struggled with his feeling that it was her fault, and managed to come through this because he saw that if he didn't overcome this feeling, their marriage would break up and then he would have "lost everything that mattered to him." He and Maureen both cried as he said this.

4. The Jacksons are more noticeably reticent than the others in participating. In one or two exchanges between this couple, I have the impression that there is some disagreement between them as to whether Anne might have survived if they had got her to the hospital emergency room sooner. David told the group, "It didn't seem any worse than so many of the attacks we'd pulled her through before," but Moira had said rather sharply that she'd "realized right away it was different from the others." David had looked down at his hands but had not responded. When Katherine Parker suggested to Moira that the care of such a severely handicapped child as Anne must have been very difficult indeed, Moira replied, almost angrily, "You do what you have to do. The child didn't ask to come into the world like that."

CHAPTER 24

Group Work: Roseland Park Seniors Club

Agency:
Family Service Center, Aged and Aging Services, Lakesford (pop. 150,000)

Referral date:
March 4, 19xx.

Referral source:
Club members Mrs. K. Bukevic and Mr. G. Mason.

Background

The Seniors Club was formed four years ago at the Roseland Park Retirement Community, which is managed by the Lakesford Housing Authority. Tenants pay rent geared to their income. Our services to the aged and aging provide social work service to elderly residents on a purchase-of-service agreement with the Housing Authority. I had been involved originally in getting the club organized, in response to a request from a Housing Authority manager who had been approached about this. I had met Mrs. Bukevic at that time, but not Mr. Mason.

First Interview

These two people came to my office by appointment to discuss the Roseland Park Seniors Club. They stated that they represented others in the club, but did not wish to "name any names." Mrs. Bukevic is widowed; Mr. Mason's wife has just had cataract surgery, "otherwise she'd certainly be here with me," he said.

Both are very concerned about what is happening to the club.

Since its formation four years ago, the established pattern has been that the recreation room has been available for the members' use from 10:30 a.m. to 5:00 p.m. every Wednesday. On the third Wednesday of each month, social get togethers are held in the evening. Each member may invite one guest to any of these activities and some of these guests have become "regulars," some joining the club (permitted by a motion of the club membership), and others paying a small fee each time they attend.

The Wednesday daytime activities are usually quite informal: card games, pool, and other table games put together on the spot, or by arrangement, between individual members. Once a month the public health nurse comes to take members' blood pressure and give advice on general health. On some occasions, she, or an appropriate colleague, gives a short talk on medical subjects that may be of interest to the members such as menus for diabetics, cooking for heart health, exercises for keeping fit, and so on.

I asked how these topics were chosen and both Mrs. Bukevic and Mr. Mason said they felt this was part of the trouble. The public health nurse simply announces each month if there will be a talk the following month and states the topic. Sometimes some of the members have no interest in these talks, and they feel that their free activity time is restricted because they must either listen or stay home. Mrs. Bukevic feels that the talks are often more like "lectures on how to behave" and the members resent this, but Mr. Mason said he believes that more members would accept these events if they felt they had some say in what topics were to be scheduled. He laughed and said, "It's a bit like your mother telling you, 'Eat this, it's good for you.' If she didn't say that, you might get to like the stuff!"

I asked if they had brought this concern to the Club Committee, and they said that one member had raised it at a general meeting, but the president, Mrs. McFarlane, had said the club was very lucky to have the opportunity to hear these talks, and it would be inappropriate for them to start telling the public health people their job. They (the public health people) were the professionals and were ready to share their expert information, and "We should realize how privileged we are here in Lakesford." I wondered whether anyone had tried to support the member who had raised the issue, but Mrs. Bukevic said angrily, "No one wants to speak up against the McFarlanes—they act like they're the boss of everything and everyone bows to them."

She went on to explain that Mr. and Mrs. McFarlane moved into the community a year ago January from Jamesville, five hundred miles away. They wanted to be near their son and his family who live here in Lakesford. The son is a successful lawyer—"as we're reminded every other minute." The McFarlanes became active in the club "as soon as they had their curtains up," and by the spring elections quite a few of the members were sufficiently impressed that they were "real workers" and they elected Mrs. McFarlane president, and her husband—a retired bank manager—treasurer. Mr. Mason said that ever since the fall, "it doesn't feel like *our* club anymore." Asked to explain, he said the McFarlanes just "run things" in their own way, and no one else has any say anymore.

Mrs. Bukevic said, for example, "On Wednesday evenings, we used to make our own fun, but since the McFarlanes took over, it's all concerts and 'highfalutin' stuff." Mr. Mason said that anything the members suggest is either just quietly dropped, or they (the McFarlanes) "wangle it around" so it seems as if it would not be sufficiently popular.

Mr. Mason said one member had suggested that it would be interesting to have the McFarlanes' son come and talk to them about making a will, but Mrs. McFarlane had really put him down, saying that a successful lawyer was *far* too busy and she couldn't think of asking him to do such a thing "for charity." Mr. McFarlane had expressed surprise that there would be anyone in the club who hadn't made a will. The ones who hadn't or who had let theirs get out-of-date were ashamed to speak up after that. Mr. Mason said that he felt sorry for those members because, "It's like they (the McFarlanes) feel we're not in their class," he said, adding, "Well, maybe we aren't, but we've got feelings."

Mrs. Bukevic said that once, some members had suggested they would like to have a sing-along with national songs from their respective "old countries." There are a couple of residents who play the piano well, and this activity was agreed upon. When the evening came, the McFarlanes and "their clique" stayed away, so that some of the pleasure was taken away from the evening. Later several members heard that the McFarlanes had said they weren't interested in "that sort of thing," and the members who had arranged it felt put down and were quite hurt by this.

A decided "split" has come about in the club because of what has happened, and it has made for hard feelings between former friends who have taken opposite sides on the issue of the McFarlanes' methods.

Mrs. Bukevic said that attendance has fallen off noticeably on Wednesday evenings, and some of the guests who used to attend regularly tell their hosts and hostesses that, while they miss coming, the monthly programs are not interesting to them anymore.

The annual meeting will be the last week of May and elections will have to be held. Unless the members are prepared to speak up about how they feel, a lot of members will just stay away, and the club will be in danger of folding. Mrs. Bukevic and Mr. Mason have tried to get some of the dissatisfied members to organize and speak up to the McFarlanes, but most say they don't want to cause a fight, and would rather let their membership go for the sake of peace. However, a few did say they thought it was a good idea to come to our agency to see if we could help.

I asked if Mr. and Mrs. McFarlane had been told of this move, but both Mrs. Bukevic and Mr. Mason said no, they had been afraid to tell them themselves. They did not mind, however, if I mentioned their names in broaching the matter, either at the club or with the McFarlanes, because they felt someone had to stand up and be counted for the good of the club. They did know of some others who would support them if they felt it was "safe" to do so. By this they meant if I was there to assist.

I promised that I would first clear with the Housing Authority and our agency that it was permissible for me to get involved, adding that I felt it was appropriate that they had asked for help and I had no doubt that approval would be given. I would think over very carefully just how it would be best for me to approach the issues, being concerned not to make things worse for the members, who after all, have to live together in relatively close quarters whatever happens to the club. I added that perhaps the McFarlanes do have something to contribute to the club, if they can come to see that it is important that other members' opinions and wishes be respected.

PART SIX

MEDICAL AND VOCATIONAL
SOCIAL SERVICES

CHAPTER 25

Post-Traumatic Stress Syndrome: Marvin Thompson[1]

Agency:

Veteran's Administration Hospital, Outpatient Services, Morganville (pop. 100,000)

Referral date:

October 26, 19xx.

Referral source:

Dr. P. E. Marriott, psychiatrist at the Greenvale Addiction Center.

Client:

Marvin Thompson, age 42, born June 24, 19xx, divorced, no contact with family members.

An appointment was made with Mr. Thompson by phone for November 1st. He phoned in the morning and left a message with the receptionist that he was unable to make it and would call me. He called again on November 7th and made an appointment for November 9th, which he did not keep. On November 28th, he called again, and I spoke with him. He said he had thought the psychiatrist had been making a "big thing" of some of the things he (Mr. Thompson) had told her, but that now he was feeling "scared" and thought he had better talk to someone before he "goes crazy." We made an appointment for November 30th.

The following material actually was obtained in two interviews,

1. This case was written by Lola West, L.C.S.W., Coordinator, Adult Day Health Care Program, V.A. Medical Center, Little Rock, AR.

but has been put together in order to simplify the chronology and for the purposes of the assessment.

Intake Interview: November 30 and December 7, 19xx

Mr. Thompson was nearly fifteen minutes late for his first interview. (He was on time for his second appointment.) He said he knew he was late, but added sarcastically that it had probably given me "time for another coffee break." He is about 5'10", with a slender build, light brown hair and fine features. I felt he looked rather grey and "drawn." He was neatly dressed and presented a generally well-groomed appearance.

He looked anxiously around the room and asked where he should sit, then chose an upright chair. He sat on the edge and appeared very anxious, wringing his hands, smoothing his sweater and pants, and rubbing his chin. As we began, he looked uneasily at the curtains on the inner wall and asked if they covered "one of those two-way mirror things." I immediately drew them back, showed him that the adjoining room was unoccupied, and told him the door to that room was locked. If he would prefer, we could talk with the drapes drawn back. He said yes, that would be better. He was used to this at Dr. Marriott's office. But he added that he supposed "all the mikes were off." I reassured him on this, and told him that I would never record our interviews without his knowledge and his written consent, as it was against the hospital's rules. He nodded agreement but said sometimes people broke the rules. His nervous hand-gestures continued.

Presenting Problem

Dr. Marriott's report, which she had shared with Mr. Thompson, indicated that he was haunted with "flashbacks" of Vietnam, sometimes actually thinking he was back there. He was also experiencing extreme guilt feelings, both about having survived—his best friend was killed beside him in an ambush—and also for things he did in Vietnam and upon his return. He has been drug-free for six months, and is employed full-time as a pipe-fitter/welder at Karlin Industries.

I told him that I realized it had been difficult for him to come here, but that Dr. Marriott believed that we could help him with some of the things that were troubling him at present. I commended him for having been six months free of his cocaine habit, and said it must have taken a lot of courage to make that kind of break. He said that although he feels good about that, he now has "more time to think" and he is afraid he is going crazy with "thinking so much about such awful things." I said we were still seeing many men whose memories of Vietnam give them bad times, and this was what I would try to help him with. He said bitterly, "I know! I'm just another screwed up 'Nam vet."

I said I was sorry if what I had said sounded as if I felt that way about him. What I meant was that he was not alone, and after what he had been through, there was no shame in needing some help to sort things out. He seemed to accept this, and went on to say that sometimes he has felt so bad he has thought of suicide, but he believes that would be cowardly. In reply to my question, he told me he had enlisted in the Navy right out of high school, when he was nineteen.

Background Information

Mr. Thompson told me that his enlistment was in emulation of his paternal grandfather, who was a WWI veteran, and had been an important person while he was growing up. He was brought up by his paternal grandparents. They told him that his parents were divorced soon after his birth and that neither of them wanted the responsibility of a baby. He has always believed there was "more to it" than that, but "it wasn't anything I could talk about." He never remembers seeing either of his parents. He enjoyed growing up on his grandparents' farm, he had his chores, and felt good about that. He did well in school and was active in all sports. He feels he was loved and encouraged as a child, had lots of friends, and never got into any trouble, other than boyish pranks. He was very close to his grandfather, who sometimes spoke about his wartime experiences and said he hoped Marvin would never have to go through that. But he had also sometimes expressed the conviction that "a man must be ready to die for his country."

Mr. Thompson had been in the Navy less than a year when he was ordered to Vietnam in 1968.

Combat Experiences

In Vietnam, he was assigned to river boat patrols, a particularly vulnerable activity. He became terrified of river patrols after having three boats shot out from under him with loss of life and serious injuries to friends. He thought he would be safer on land patrol, and he applied and was allowed to transfer. He persuaded his best friend, Jim, to transfer with him. He feels very guilty because, as he sees it, he "really pushed" Jim to transfer. Jim was later killed while on land patrol.

It was during one of his first land patrols that Mr. Thompson had his first experience with acts of atrocity. Walking into a village that had been attacked by the Viet Cong, his first sight was of a young Vietnamese woman, hanging suspended with her fetus cut from her body but left attached. This horrified him so much that his fear became almost overwhelming. "I had never thought of people doing things like that to other people. It was just so awful." Following on the heels of this came ambushes, firefights, finding mutilated American soldiers, and the death of his best friend.

Jim was killed as the squad returned from a two-day patrol. The squad had felt that someone was following them so they performed a search but found nothing amiss. Jim and Mr. Thompson were the last two men in line as the squad moved out. After once more reconnoitering the area, they knelt facing each other ("Just inches apart," Mr. Thompson said.) As they held a whispered discussion of their findings, a shot was fired, and Jim slumped forward with a fatal wound to his head.

Mr. Thompson sat silent, looking at his hands, which he clasped and unclasped continually. I waited with him, and then I said, "Do you want to tell me about it?" He almost writhed in pain as he told me that he shook Jim and slapped him and "I screamed at him for dying. It was an awful thing to do, the guy was dead, and I yelled at him." Mr. Thompson cried for a few moments, then regained his composure and went on to explain that the Medivac chopper couldn't get in to remove Jim's body, so Mr. Thompson carried him through the jungle himself. "I couldn't leave him there. Some of the guys wanted to take a turn to help me, but I said no, Jim was my friend, I'd carry him out myself," and he added, "After what I'd done, it was the least I could do, wasn't it?" He went on to explain that when they got to the river boat that was picking them up, apparently he wouldn't let go of Jim, and someone had to pry the body from him. He didn't remember that part of it for several years. "They said it was like I was in shock and didn't know what I was doing."

After that, Mr. Thompson said, he just "went tough and like— brutal." He said it was as if he "didn't feel at all, nothing but this rage, like I was just boiling up inside all the time." Some of the guys tried to be friendly because they knew he and Jim had been real close, but "I just swore at them and told them to f--- off." He didn't want to be close to anyone, he just wanted to do anything, he said to "get back at those bastards for killing Jim." He wrung his hands together in distress as he said "I did some awful, awful things whenever I got the chance. Even some of the other guys were shocked, but I didn't listen to them." It feels awful to him now, and sometimes he wonders if it was really him doing those things, but he knows it was. "And I came out of it alive, when I saw so many others go down." He covered his face with his hands and we sat silently for a minute or so. Then he said that lots of those guys he knew would have made a better job of civilian life if they'd come home instead of him. He has hurt so many people since he came back, he often wonders why he came back alive and they didn't.

Post-Vietnam

Mr. Thompson said when he came back to the U.S. he went to a vocational/technical school, qualified as a pipe-fitter/welder, and worked at various jobs in construction and in oilfields. Although he has changed jobs a lot, he has worked steadily almost all the time since he got out of the Navy.

He met his wife on a visit home to his grandparents and they got married after a short acquaintance. She and her family were well-known to his grandparents, and it "seemed like the right thing to do." He said after they were married she complained a lot that he was cold and "not loving enough," but he just couldn't feel any loving feelings, and he thought it should be enough that he worked regularly and brought his paycheck home. When Lorraine became pregnant, "I was supposed to be happy," and at first, he hoped a child would make a difference for him, but as she began to show in pregnancy he told me he began to "see" the Vietnamese woman of his horrible memory, rather than Lorraine. He began having nightmares and became very irritable. He and Lorraine quarreled a lot. His bad temper lost him a job just before his son was born, and although he soon got another, it frightened him because he felt as if he couldn't "hold on to anything."

He began to have nightmares about hurting his little boy, and avoided being with the child as much as he could. This hurt Lorraine, and their fighting became almost continuous. Their son was barely a year old when Lorraine became pregnant again, and once more the Vietnam memory came back to him. Not long after the second baby was born (another boy), he became so agitated and easily enraged that he left the family for fear of what he might do to them. They were divorced a year later, and he has severed all connection with them because he believed that they were "better off without a crazy, mean husband and father."

After this, he went through a "bad time." He drank heavily, picked fights, and was arrested on several occasions for assaults and drunken brawls. He was never sentenced to jail, however. At one point he straightened out, with the help of a probation officer, went back to school, and got two years college credit, after which he taught welding for about two years at a vocational/technical school. It was then that his grandfather died.

Mr. Thompson said he felt that with the death of his grandfather he had "lost the only anchor in my life." His grandfather had been the only person he felt had understood him, and even when he was doing things he knew his grandfather didn't approve of, he felt sure that he could go to Grandpa, who would certainly bawl him out, but would never give up on him.

I asked how he had coped with his grandfather's death—he must have felt very much alone at that time. He told me he had taken his dog and gone to live in the woods in a deserted shack he had found while walking one day. "I felt, what's the use of getting to need other people when you only lose them anyway?" he said. He lived this hermit existence for over a year. Then he went back to work in Keenesville and got into a crowd that was into drugs. He told me that he sort of "woke up" one day after he spent another night in jail for drunken fighting, and came home to find his dog hungry and sort of sick. He said maybe it sounded weird to me but the way his dog greeted him— so loving "in spite of what I'd done"—made him think about what kind of a person he was. It was then that he decided to get treatment for his drug addiction.

I explained that I would like to help him with the things that were making it so tough for him and that here at the hospital we worked on a contract basis. To be helpful, I would need to see him every week on a regular basis, and I thought we should agree on eight weeks to start with. At the end of that time we could look together at where things were with him. I also gave him our "Lifeline" emergency number that he can call at any time, day or night, if things get bad for him. I told him also that some of our patients had found it helpful if, in addition to the personal counseling, they joined a small group of Vietnam vets to share their feelings, and that this would be open to him at some time if he felt it would be of help to him. He said he didn't like that idea at all. How could you trust other people to understand, and not to "blab your story all over town?" He added that he "guessed he had to trust (me)." Dr. Marriott had told him that "you would be out on your ear" if I ever told anyone outside the hospital about what he had told me. I said that was right. Mr. Thompson repeated that he guessed he had to trust someone, because he really wants to "be normal" and he doesn't want to go on "hurting people," like he has hurt so many people in his life. He wants to be a "good man like my grandfather."

We contracted a series of eight weekly appointments and when he left after the second interview he told me he felt he "could sort of get used to coming to see me, in time." I told him I hoped that he would find it helped him.

CHAPTER 26

AIDS: Kyle Muldoon[1]

Agency:
Community Mental Health Services in a medium-sized industrial city (pop. 500,000).

Referral source:
Self, Kyle Muldoon, by phone.

Referral date:
March 3, 19xx.

Family data:
Father: Patrick Muldoon, age 59.
Mother: Elizabeth Muldoon, age 54.
Siblings: Maureen, age 33.
Kerry, dd. 19xx at age 16.
Kyle, age 29.
Kathleen, age 26.
Patricia, age 24.

Intake interview:
March 10, 19xx.

Presenting Problem

Kyle, age twenty-nine, asked for help with "frequent anxiety attacks." These began about six weeks ago and have gradually been increasing in frequency and intensity. His supervisor suggested that he needed

1. This case was written by Patricia Millar, L.C.S.W., Case Manager, Domiciliary Homeless Program, V.A. Medical Center, Little Rock, AR.

professional counseling, as lately these have been occurring at work. He is a C.P.A., working for the past five years with a firm of accountants who recently—as of January 1st of this year—expanded to incorporate two other, smaller firms in the city. He told me that his supervisor, who seems to be sensitive and understanding, had told him also that his co-workers lately find him irritable and "touchy." We arranged an appointment for March 10, 19xx.

Intake Interview: March 10, 19xx

Kyle appeared very tense and nervous at the beginning of the interview. He sat on the edge of his chair, continually rolling his fingers around on his knee. His answers to my questions were at first extremely brief and it took a little while before he was able to loosen up to tell me more about himself and what was troubling him.

He told me that upon graduating with his B.A. in business administration, he had worked for two years for General Trust, Inc., and when he achieved his C.P.A. five years ago, he began with Hoffner, Parkes, and Ephron and has been with them ever since. He really enjoys his work and feels that until very recently he has always gotten along well with his co-workers.

When I asked him about his prospects for promotion, Kyle began to cry. With some difficulty, he told me that about two months ago, having learned that a former long-term sexual partner had AIDS, he had his blood tested. The results came back indicating that Kyle is HIV positive.

He said that he is terrified. Two years ago, he spent a lot of time with another friend who was dying of AIDS and says that sometimes the fear of having to go through what he saw his friend suffer just overwhelms him. At such times, it is all he can do to remain on the job, and a couple of times recently, when with a client, he has had to excuse himself from the room, "run away" (his phrase), and hide in a stairwell until he could regain control.

Background Information

Kyle is presently in an intense, intimate, relationship with his live-in partner, Jerry, a prominent pediatrician. He has not been able to tell Jerry that he has tested HIV positive, but has abstained from sex since receiving the test results, giving numerous excuses for his abstinence.

Kyle is the third of five children. His parents live about 350 miles away in Kerryville, a community with a population of 50,000. They do not know that he is gay. Kyle said that it would simply "destroy any love they ever had" for him if they knew. In response to my noting how he had phrased this, he said that his father operates a construction business that was founded by his maternal grandfather. His parents had always assumed that when Kyle graduated, he would join the family firm. However, in his last year of high school he began to suspect he was gay, and in college he had begun to face more and more the implications of being gay in today's society. He began to feel that once he was self-supporting, he would need to get away from home. Although he had found acceptance with other gays at college and with many of his classmates, he had experienced a certain amount of verbal abuse from some, both male and female. Upon graduation, he felt that he had to find a job and live in a larger city where his gay life-style would not center him out as he believed it would in the "small-town" atmosphere of his hometown.

This decision of his had been a grave disappointment to his father, who took it as a kind of "betrayal of the family," and as a reflection on himself as a father. Kyle said his dad thought others would believe Kyle felt the family business was "beneath him" and that by choosing not to work with his dad, Kyle was implying that he and his father did not get along. Kyle had tried to reassure his dad that this was not the case but, of course, he was unable to tell him the real reason. His father and mother remain deeply hurt by his decision.

Kyle's family is quite prominent in their home community. His father is very musical and plays the organ and trains the choir in his church. His mother is a nurse, and after staying home with the five children during their early years, she returned to work outside the home and now nurses part-time in a retirement and long-term care residential facility in Kerryville. Both of them are very active in community affairs.

Kyle is the third of five children. The eldest is a girl, now married and living here in Middlesford. The second child was a boy, Kerry, who died at age sixteen of leukemia. Kyle was then thirteen. The two youngest children are girls. Kyle said Kerry's death was a dreadful experience for the whole family, and he feels that in some ways his parents have never recovered from it. From the time that Kerry died, but especially after he himself reached sixteen, he always felt that he didn't "qualify" as a member of the family. Asked to explain this, he said that he felt that he was "supposed to make it up to them" for Kerry's death, but that he could never measure up to their memory of the "Golden Boy." For example, although his school marks were always very good, they were never quite good enough to satisfy his parents. Getting into a fight in junior high was described by his parents as something Kerry would "never have done." Kerry had played piano and guitar, and sang in the choir, but Kyle is not at all musical. Although his youngest sister is not musical either, it was always Kyle's lack of musical ability that was "rubbed in" by his parents. His realization of being gay seemed to him the final, damning confirmation of not belonging in the family.

He has always been close to his eldest sister, Maureen, who is four years older than him. She is the only one of his family who knows he is gay. He gets along well with her husband, and visits with them fairly often. It was the only place, he said, where he didn't have to hide anything—"I could be *me*," he said sadly. I pointed out his use of the past tense and he explained that even that is changed now, because he can't bring himself to tell her that he has tested positive for the HIV virus.

He only visits his parents about once or twice a year. He uses the excuse that he has to work a lot of overtime, and also that his volunteer involvement with a sports program for physically challenged children takes a lot of his time on weekends. His parents sometimes complain about this when he phones them and his father invariably mentions that people in the community were asking after him and "wondering when he was coming home to visit." In addition, his father often says things that imply that Kyle has grown too much the "big-city business man" to be bothered with "small-town folks."

Kyle finds this very difficult to cope with. It hurts him that his father "gets at him" like this. At the same time, it makes it all the more difficult for him to visit home since he knows the same attitude will be there, both openly and "in the atmosphere." He feels in a bind about all of this and doesn't think there is any way to resolve the issue of his relationship with his parents.

He is terrified of losing Jerry, but realizes that he will have to tell him eventually about his HIV test result. He is scared that Maureen and her husband will not want him around either, fearing for themselves and their two small children. He is terrified that he will be abandoned "if and when I get sick and unable to care for myself." At times he feels like he is drowning or "being swallowed up from the inside."

He said that although he had felt very scared coming here, on the whole it was a relief to talk about it to someone. However, he cannot see any way out of all the complications involved in the situation. He has thought of cashing in all his savings and "finding a cabin in the mountains somewhere" where he could just live by himself and not have to deal with anyone else.

CHAPTER 27

Medical Social Services:
Frank Bertollini

Agency:
> Social Services Department, Cameronsville General Hospital.

Referral date:
> December 2, 19xx.

Referral source:
> Interdisciplinary committee consisting of psychiatrist, M.D. specialist, nurse, physiotherapist, occupational therapist, and social worker.

Patient:
> Frank Bertollini, age 58, born August 21, 19xx. Admitted to hospital, November 20, for an undetermined length of stay for preparatory treatment prior to being fitted for an artificial limb. He will remain here for a period after that for training in wearing the prosthesis.

Family data:
> *Wife:* Angela Bertollini, age 54, born May 8, 19xx.
> *Children:* Mario, age 25, married, 2 children, living in Steeltown, 500 miles away.
>> Donna-Marie, age 24, married, 1 child, living in Baysville, 90 miles away.
>> Frank, Jr., age 22, married, no children, wife, Darlene, living in Cameronsville.

Background Information

Mr. Bertollini was first interviewed alone on December 4, 19xx. The second interview occurred on December 7, 19xx, with both Mr. and

Mrs. Bertollini. Mr. Bertollini was injured in an accident at work which crushed his left foot and the lower part of his leg. Doctors were unable to save the limb and he had to have his left leg amputated below the knee. This was in late August. He returned home in mid-September, and remained at home until the recent readmission. During the post-operative period at home, Mr. Bertollini was cared for by Home Care Services. The visiting nurse did dressings and advised them about general care.

They cashed a couple of bonds and bought some of the necessary equipment, such as bars for the bathroom, crutches, and a bathtub stool. Mario and his wife gave them a hand-held shower so that Mr. Bertollini could bathe himself. At present they are using a wheelchair on loan from Home Care. Mr. Bertollini can drive, but transportation for his wife to the hospital is difficult. Mrs. Bertollini does not drive and their home is about seventeen miles out of the city. Their daughter-in-law, Darlene, is very helpful and drives her into town once, and sometimes more frequently, during the week. Frank and Darlene also bring her to church every Sunday.

The Bertollinis own their own home, but they feel they cannot remain there because of the stairs. After the surgery, Mr. Bertollini slept on a bed in the dining room, and his wife slept upstairs. Mr. Bertollini is a big man and it was very awkward for him to go up and down the stairs during that period. Both felt this separation keenly, and have been thinking about how to manage when Mr. Bertollini comes home again. They are reluctant to give up their home, but realize that on several counts they may have to consider this. It would appear that they would do better in an apartment with some modifications, so that Mr. Bertollini can use a wheelchair until he becomes completely comfortable with his prosthesis.

Financial Factors

Mr. Bertollini has recently been granted a full pension by his former employer (Cosgrove's Mining Equipment). Mrs. Bertollini used to work part-time at the Park Street Nursing Home, but when Mr. Bertollini came home after surgery she could not continue, and is not working outside the home at the present time. His pension is, of course, less than his working income, and they are worried about how they will manage.

Although 75 percent of the cost of the preparatory prosthesis is covered by the Assistive Devices program, the amount of their required contribution is—for them—a considerable sum, which is at present beyond their means.[1] They don't want to ask their children to help out.

1. These costs will vary with state or private medical insurance plans.

Adjustment to Loss

Mr. Bertollini was an active athlete in his youth. He was an ardent golfer and, up until the accident, still managed to play racquetball once a week during the winter. He feels the loss of his limb keenly and reports that he is "just not myself any more." He has periods of depression, and at these times he just stares at the TV all the time. He admits that when he is feeling this way, "Angie has to watch that I don't drink too much."

He said he feels at times it might have been better if he had been killed in the accident than to be left "only half a man." Mrs. Bertollini's reaction to this statement, which was made to me in her presence, was briskly businesslike and nonemotional. "Now *that*," she said, "we'll never know, and here you are and we've got to make the best of it." Mr. Bertollini laughed ruefully and said to me that I could see he didn't get much sympathy from her. Mrs. Bertollini laughed a little also, took his hand, and said she'd rather have him here with one good leg than not have him here at all. I noticed that her eyes were full of tears in spite of her brisk, half-humorous manner.

Alone with me, Mr. Bertollini told me that Mrs. Bertollini is still unable to look at his stump and that when she helps him in or out of the bathtub and so on, she averts her eyes. This makes him "feel terrible" he says, because the nurses are trying to help him face the fact that it will always be there. When his wife turns away from it, he feels he has somehow let her down, "Like I'm not good enough for her any more." He said she has always been "the strong one" when times were rough before.

CHAPTER 28

Medical Social Services: Joanne Cassell

Agency:
Hospital Social Services in a medium-sized industrial city (pop. 125,000)

Referral date:
November 29, 19xx.

Referral source:
Nursing staff, dialysis unit.

Client:
Joanne Cassell, age 23, born October 23, 19xx. Lives at home.

Family data:
   Father: John Cassell, deceased
   Mother: Jean Cassell, age 65
   Siblings: Marvin, age 33, married, lives and works in Steeltown, 300 miles away.
         Lorraine, age 32, single, lives at home, works as cook in local retirement home.
         Frances, age 29, single parent, living at home with six-month-old baby.

Presenting Problem

Joanne will require dialysis three times a week. She was diagnosed as a diabetic at age seven, and her mother states that at that time the doctor told her she had very little time to live, and the family should make that time as easy and pleasant for her as possible. Kidney failure was brought on by her persistent noncompliance with the dietary and insulin regimen prescribed as necessary to control the diabetes. At age seventeen she began to experience some very gradual loss of vision, also caused by the noncompliance.

Transportation

Joanne sees this as her only real problem. The family lives in a very small rural community about four miles out of Birchville. A bus stop for Birchville is located about a mile from their home, and from Birchville a bus runs hourly to Cameronsville, connecting with a Handi-Transit service to the hospital. There is no taxi service from the family home to the bus stop for Birchville, and there is no family car.

At the present time, an unemployed young neighbor is driving Joanne and her mother to Birchville to get the bus for town, but this young man has recently applied to enter a retraining program, so this arrangement will not last much longer.

For some patients where transportation is a problem, a system of continuous peritoneal dialysis is considered, whereby they can remain at home, but this requires strictly sterile technique. This cannot be recommended in Joanne's case because of her very low standard of personal hygiene.

Patient Care Issues

At home, she absolutely refuses to take a shower. She occasionally soils herself en route to the bathroom, because her bowel-bladder control is very slightly impaired at times. However, she is careless about cleaning herself up and washing her hands, and strongly resists changing her underwear following such accidents. She is slovenly in all areas of personal grooming. When at home, provided she agrees, her mother or oldest sister will bathe her in the tub. They wash her hair, again when she agrees, in the kitchen sink, because the placement of facilities in the family bathroom makes it impossible to use the wash-basin for this. There is no physical reason why she could not wash her own hair. Her mother and sister simply do not have the strength to insist that these cleanliness routines be carried out regularly—or even weekly. They cannot handle Joanne's tantrums and give up the struggle if she resists their suggestions.

When hospitalized, Joanne is a very difficult patient indeed. She is demanding of the nurses, and cannot tolerate any degree of frustration. She cries and goes into tantrums when she is thwarted in any way. For example, if the Handi-Transit bus is later than usual to take her to the bus terminal, she cries bitterly and on one occasion shouted (in the hospital lobby) that no one cared about her—she could die right there and no one would give a damn, etc., all at the top of her lungs.

As an inpatient she seems to believe or feel that she should not be required to do anything for herself. She resists getting out of bed, refuses to take a shower, although there is no reason why she could not do so with a nurse present. She wants the nurse to wash her face and hands, etc.

Other Background Information

Mrs. Cassell, is a small, thin, very nervous-appearing woman, who is currently on tranquilizers prescribed by her doctor. Mr. Cassell was an alcoholic and died of a massive heart attack five years ago. Joanne has told one of the nurses that her mother is also an alcoholic but does not drink now. Mrs. Cassell told me that at home, Joanne watches TV all the time in her pajamas and dressing gown, and insists that her meals be brought to her on a tray in the family living room.

Family income is minimal. Mrs. C. receives a small pension from the railway where Mr. C. was employed for forty years, and she also receives Social Security. Lorraine's earnings help the family. Frances receives Aid to Families with Dependent Children, but this is modified as she is living at home. Joanne receives a disability pension.

Observations

I was with Mrs. C. and Joanne one day when the Handi-Transit bus was a little late, and Joanne had a tantrum. Her mother fussed around her with meek little exclamations of, "There, now" and "Never mind, dear," patting her on the shoulder and so on. I noticed that she didn't say anything reassuring (such as "The bus has never been seriously late" or "We know the connection time for the Birchville bus") but only attempted to "comfort" or quiet Joanne's distress.

Occasionally Mrs. C. expresses herself in ways that reveal how burdened she feels, although outwardly she always implies that Joanne's care is her duty, and "God's will." She told me her doctor says her "nerves are shot" and that he (the doctor) does not know how she has carried on all these years. Of course, she added quickly "Joanne's sickness is not her fault, and you people are doing all you can, I know that," and she added "I know it's your job to see to it that she gets everything."

CHAPTER 29

Vocational Rehabilitation:
Edward (Ted) Barton

Agency:
Vocational Rehabilitation Services, Lakesford (pop. 150,000)

Referral date:
October 31, 19xx.

Referral source:
Self, Mr. Barton, by phone.

Family data:
      Client: Edward (Ted) Barton, age 45, born 19xx.
        Wife: Margaret, age 43, born 19xx.
  Children: Andrew (Andy), age 17, born May 8th, 19xx.
               Lisa, age 14, born September 16th, 19xx.
               Merrilee, age 12, born January 23rd, 19xx.

Intake Interview: November 9, 19xx

Mrs. Barton accompanied her husband to the interview although Mr. Barton had not said that she would do so when he had phoned for an appointment. When he introduced us he added that it was all right for her to participate, "since the whole thing is her idea anyway."

Presenting Problem

Mr. Barton's right leg was severely injured in a mining accident two years ago, and he now walks, with some difficulty, with an elbow crutch-cane. When he first came out of the hospital and was undergoing physical therapy he believed he would be able to go back to work at the mine. In January of this year he was told by his doctors that this would not be possible and he would always need the crutch-cane. He became very depressed, and in Mrs. Barton's words, "just gave up on everything." He sits around the house all day and is bad tempered with her and the children. Mr. Barton said, "My life is just about over, sometimes I feel like the family would be better off if I was dead."

Mrs. Barton said she had talked to him about Vocational Services after she had talked to a woman at work (they work at Magnum Electric in products testing). This woman's son had gone through our services after a severe back injury. He had retrained as a welder and was now working at the iron works in Cameronsville.

For a long time Mr. Barton had refused to consider it. He felt it was hopeless in his case, because he only had a ninth grade education and was "so crippled."

This past June, their son Andy had told his parents he was quitting school to take a job at Carson's Auto Parts in the warehouse. Both of them had been very distressed at this since he was doing very well in his last year of high school at the time and planning to attend college to study geology. Mr. Barton said, with tears in his eyes, that he "hated to see the kid's dreams blown away all because of me."

Both admitted that it was at Mrs. Barton's insistence that he had contacted us, and he said he did it to please her, and (half smiling) "to put an end to her going on about it." He said I could probably convince her that at his age there was no prospect of his being retrained for any other kind of work. Two or three times he referred to himself as "a cripple."

Observations

Mr. Barton is about six feet tall and very thin. His face is deeply lined and almost haggard-looking. At first sight I thought he looked ill. He was unshaven and, although his shirt was clean, he wore an ill-fitting jacket and pants and presented a shabby, almost down-at-the-heels appearance. His dark brown hair is greying slightly at the temples.

Mrs. Barton is about 5'6", with blonde hair and round features. She presented a neatly dressed, well-groomed appearance.

I noticed that as they talked she often reached out to touch her husband's arm, but he never moved in response.

Background Information

Mr. Barton was the oldest boy in a family of eight children. His father was a factory worker and a heavy drinker, who, although he worked steadily and supported his family at a minimal level, made the family life miserable with his bad temper and physical abuse of the children. They learned early on to stay out of his way on weekends when he was drinking. As the children got older, he harped continually on what it was costing to feed them and keep them in school. He singled out Mr. Barton in particular who, at fifteen, was already six feet tall, and according to his father, "looked like a man," but "found it nice and easy to remain tied to his mother's apron strings."

Mr. Barton had wanted to take drafting at school and get a trade, but at fifteen he couldn't stand it any longer and had run away from home. He got odd jobs here and there, until at age eighteen he went underground in the mine. He met Mrs. Barton through a friend, and they were married twenty-one years ago.

Mrs. Barton had grown up on a farm, and was the eldest of four children. Her mother had died when she was sixteen years old, and she and her father had kept the home together, though he had insisted she stay in school. When she was eighteen and working in a textile factory, her father had remarried, and she had moved into town on her own. She remains in close touch with her father and stepmother, who was always very good to her and the younger children. They have now sold the farm and have moved to a retirement village at Lakesville.

Currently, all three Barton children are doing well in school. They have persuaded Andy to complete high school and he is working at Carson's Auto on Saturdays. Mrs. Barton spoke proudly of Lisa's success in public speaking contests across the city and at regional competitions. The only time I noticed any spark of positive reaction in Mr. Barton was when he reiterated Mrs. Barton's remark that the teachers find Merrilee very gifted in art. "She can draw anything," he said, "even when she was a little kid."

CHAPTER 30

Vocational Rehabilitation: Melanie Cameron

Agency:

Vocational Rehabilitation Services in a medium-sized city (pop. 125,000).

Referral date:

October 27, 19xx.

Referral source:

Self (Ms. Cameron), by phone, on the advice of Dr. Kevin O'Halloran, a psychiatrist at General Hospital, where Ms. Cameron had been hospitalized for depression for three months.

Personal data:

Melanie Cameron, age 23, born August 18, 19xx.

Intake interview:

November 9, 19xx, with Ms. Cameron.

Presenting Problem

Ms. Cameron was admitted to the hospital on June 25th, having taken an overdose of sleeping pills. The week before she had tried to cut one of her wrists with a scissors while at her desk at work. She had become hysterical and was taken home, where her mother put her to bed and made light of the incident as "a bid for attention" and yet another sign of her daughter's "lack of backbone" in the face of trouble. However, after the overdose, her condition was sufficiently alarming that her parents had driven her to the hospital and she was admitted.

She is now discharged and wants to work. However, she is very apprehensive about going back to work at her previous employment,

Reidinger's Products, where she was a computer operator in the financial department. First, she is afraid everyone will look at her and wonder when she is going to "go crazy again." Second, she would really like to go back to school, finish high school, and get a certificate in Early Childhood Education so that she can "become a kindergarten teacher."

She is afraid of going out socially and, since her discharge, has not gone out with or made any attempt to contact her former friendship group. She is worried about how they would respond because of her "craziness." Her mother has not told any of their friends or neighbors about the real nature of her illness because, "Gossip soon gets around, and your father and I have always been able to hold our heads up in this place." They told people she was visiting an aunt in Great Britain.

Background Information

The family lives in a small town about fifty miles from here where her father runs a hardware store. Her one older brother (Michael, age twenty-six) works in Highville, the state capital.

The reason for the depression was the death of a friend in a car accident. There were three of them (including Ms. Cameron) in the car at the time, returning from a party. Because her girlfriend's fiance had had to leave the party early to go to work on the nightshift, Ms. Cameron and her boyfriend had offered to drive the girl home. Ms. Cameron had had too much to drink and her boyfriend and the other girl put her in the back seat to sleep. Her boyfriend was driving. It was raining hard and an oncoming truck lost control on a curve and hit them almost head-on. Her boyfriend was badly hurt but is recovering, but the girl in the passenger seat, where, but for her condition, Ms. Cameron would have been sitting, was killed instantly.

Ms. Cameron told me that her parents, though they expressed relief that she wasn't killed, were shocked that she was in the back seat because of her drinking. They have been quite impatient with her bouts of crying and distress. Her mother feels that "pulling yourself together" is the answer to any kind of difficult feeling or event, and she has little sympathy for "weakness" or "lack of backbone."

Ms. Cameron feels that her parents are treating her as if she was still "sick." They do not want her to go out of the house without them, and if she wakes up in the night and goes to the bathroom, her mother gets up also, "just to make sure you're not getting any more funny ideas." This is very difficult for Ms. Cameron as Dr. O'Halloran has told her she must think of herself as getting well and needs to begin living a normal life.

I explained to Ms. Cameron that before we could go any further, the agency would require a medical report from Dr. O'Halloran and the hospital, and she readily signed consent forms for this purpose. Her family physician will also be contacted for verification of her current dosage of medication. In anticipation that this would not take very long, we made an appointment for her to come in two weeks from today, so that we could talk about her choices for upgrading or employment, etc., and also her need to begin leading a normal social life.

Observations

Ms. Cameron is a slim, and, in my opinion, pretty young woman, with fine features, big brown eyes, and light brown hair, becomingly styled. She was neatly dressed in a rather conservative dark blue suit with a white tailored blouse. Her stockings and shoes were also dark blue.

She rolled a tissue around in her hand as she talked, and sat very tense and upright on the edge of her chair. I noticed that whenever she quoted her mother, she looked down at her hands in a rather curious, sidelong manner, almost like a naughty child.